New Orleans as it was.

# *New Orleans as it was.*

## *Sketchbook Drawings by Mark Andresen*

1988 – HURRICANE KATRINA

PUBLISHED BY GINGKO PRESS, 2006

Compiled and written by Mark Andresen.
Designed and edited by Rudy VanderLans.

The typeface used throughout this book is Tribute. The typographic flourishes are from a typeface called Dalliance. Both were designed by Frank Heine and are licensed and distributed by Emigre.

First published in the United States of America, 2006

First Edition

Gingko Press, Inc.
5768 Paradise Drive, Suite J
Corte Madera, CA 94925, USA
Phone: (415) 924 9615
Fax: (415) 924 9608
Email: books@gingkopress.com
www.gingkopress.com/

ISBN: 1-58423-250-1
ISBN 13: 978-1-58423-250-6

LCCN: 2006928455

Printed in Hong Kong

*I* WISH TO THANK
Greg Paul, Jack Brady, and John Powers for their generous support when it counted most; Rudy VanderLans of Emigre for helping me publish this book; and the countless thousands who endured Hurricane Katrina and who hope to rebuild a new New Orleans.

In remembrance of Collaltino (Blackie), Gaspara, and Orlando—the swans of Lafreniere Park.

This book is dedicated to Paula Stratton, my wife and muse.

*M. A.*

THIS BOOK IS NOT A EULOGY for the great city of New Orleans, even after Hurricane Katrina nearly destroyed it. Instead, it is a celebration of what it was. Hopefully it is a faithful remembrance of a quintessentially American place that was living on borrowed time for years.

An original among cities of the world.

Fire, plague, and war have each destroyed it in the past, but each time it rose again with an attitude of joyful defiance in the sound of a lone trumpet above the rooftops.

It is my hope that these sketches of our city will add to the spark of rebirth that it deserves.

— *Mark Andresen*

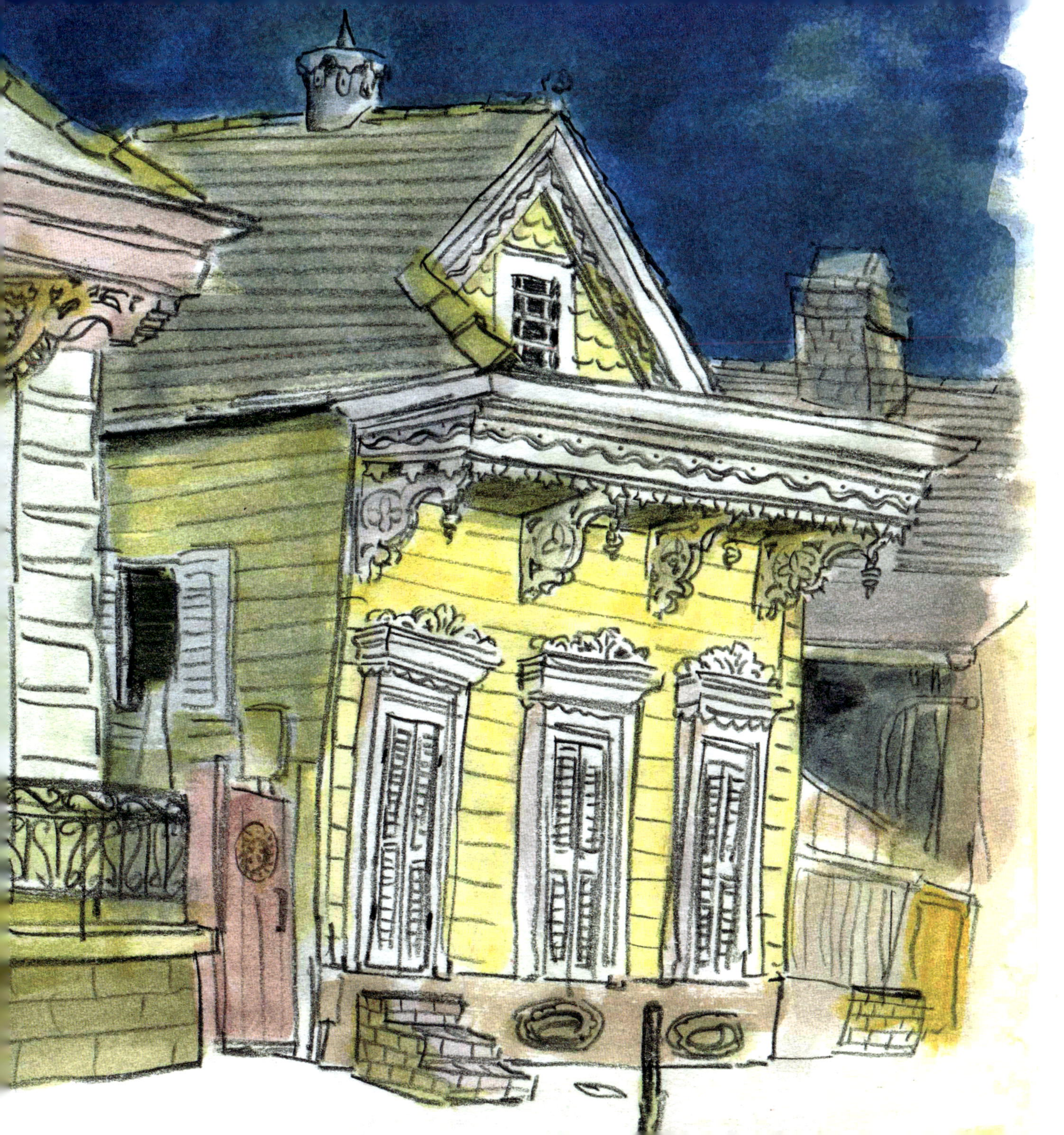

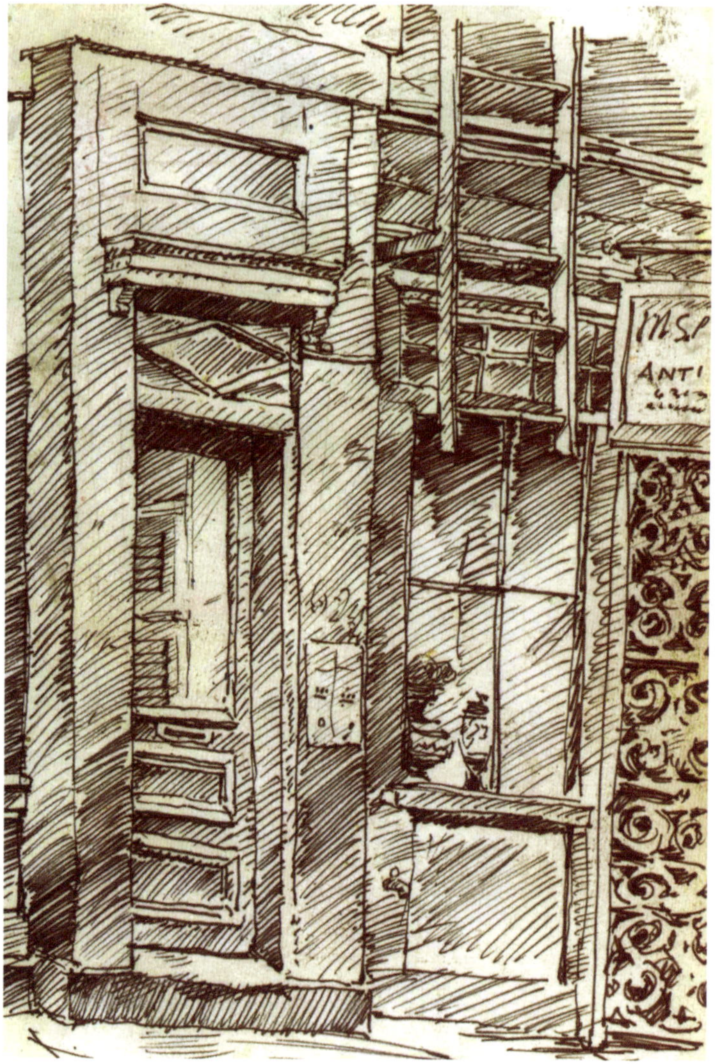


St. Peters Street.

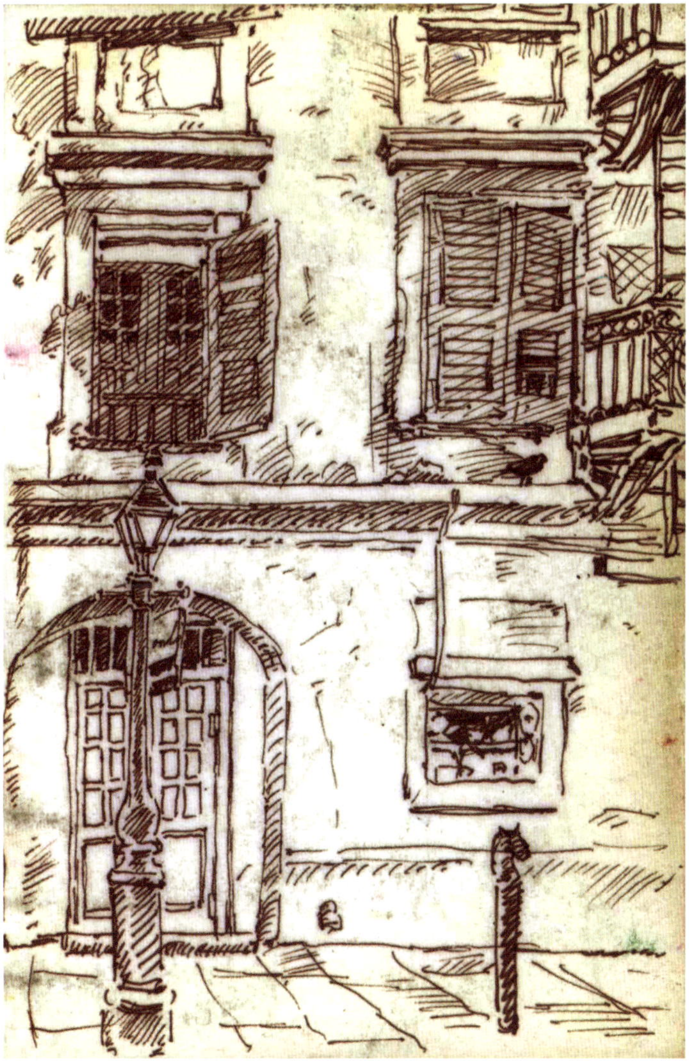

*I* FILLED UP WELL OVER A DOZEN SKETCHBOOKS during the years I lived in New Orleans. I would draw whenever I could, mostly while leaning against a wall and trying to be invisible like a ghost. Most times no one noticed me.

Sometimes, when I was scribbling, a state of grace would envelope me. There's no other way to describe this joy. Maybe it's because I love the place so much. Elegant or shabby, it didn't make any difference. Everything had a genuineness about it.

And now, after Hurricane Katrina, these memories put to paper are all I have left. So I'm giving them back to you, New Orleans—all those fleeting moments.

If I could make a solid levee of sketchbooks to protect you, I would.

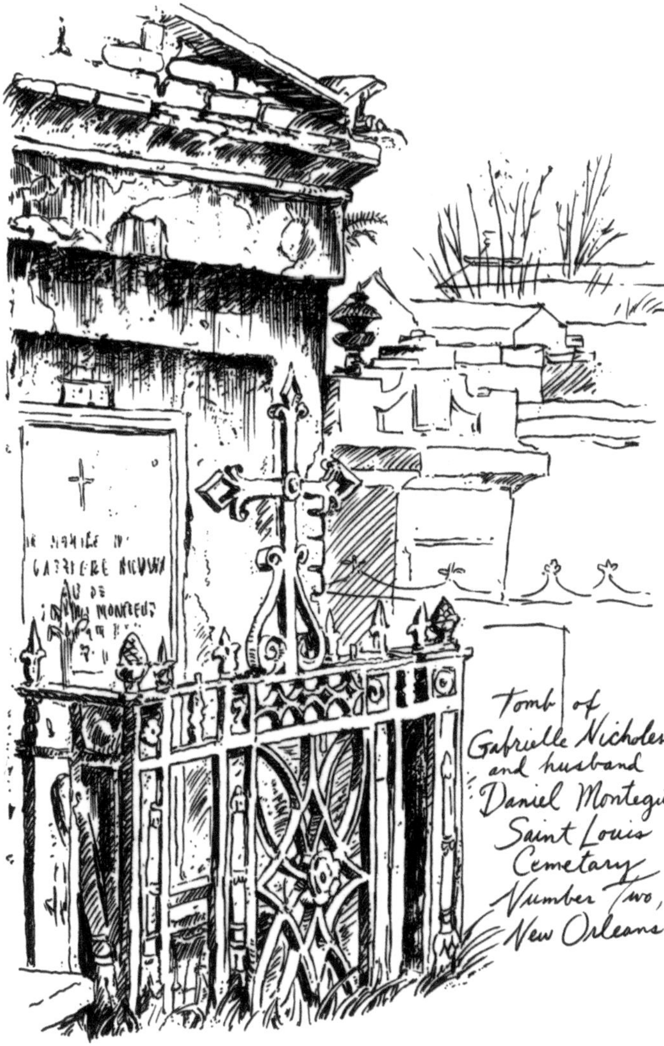

Tomb of Gabrielle Nicholes and husband Daniel Montegut, Saint Louis Cemetary Number Two, New Orleans

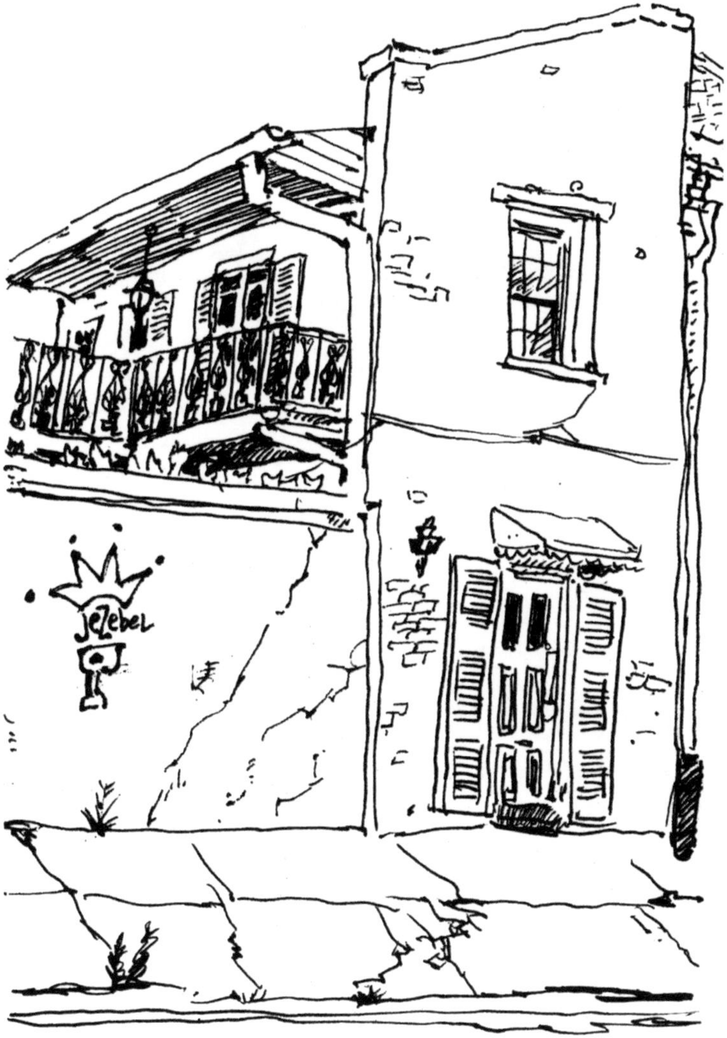


Graffiti on the wall says "Jezebel's returned."

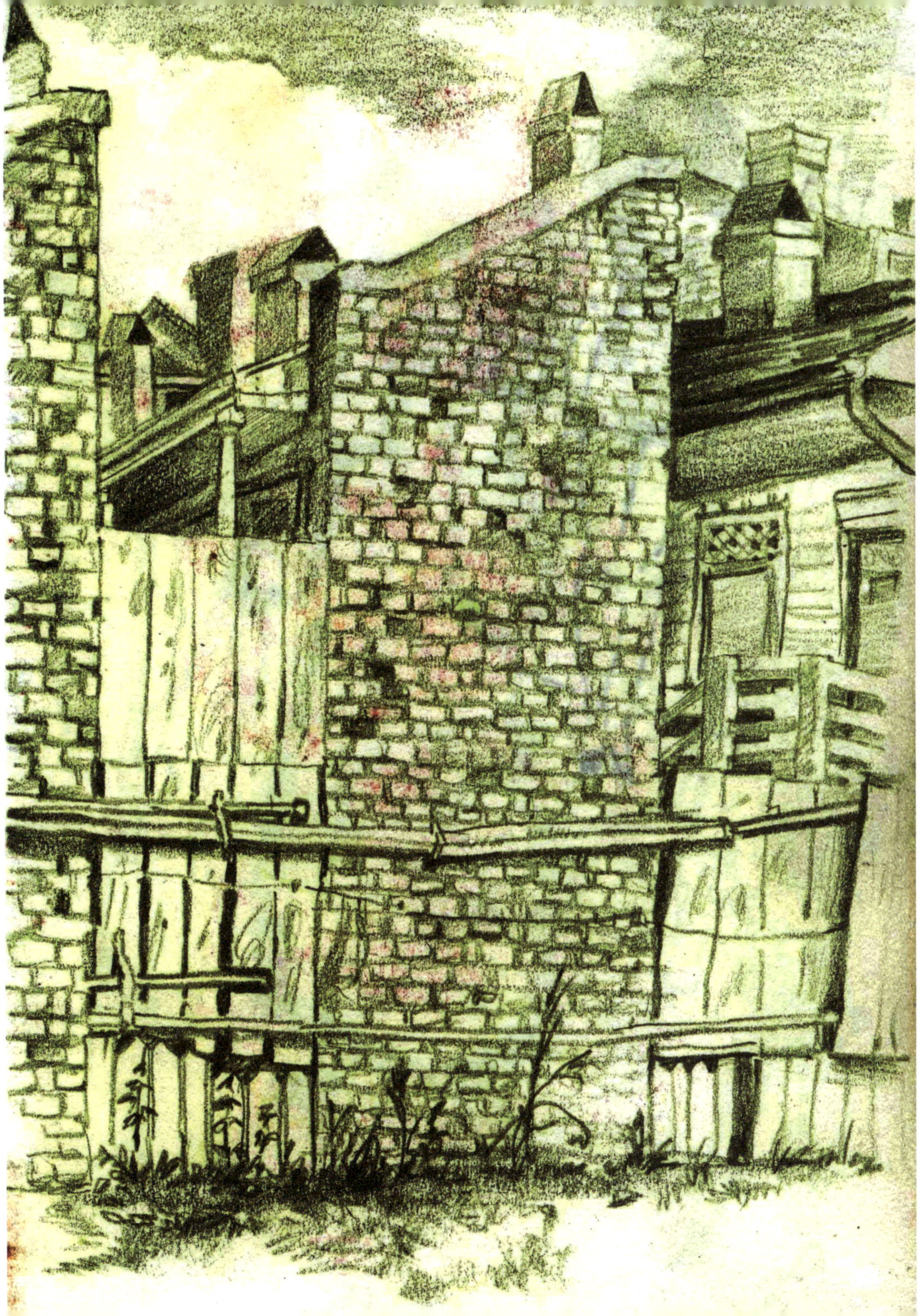

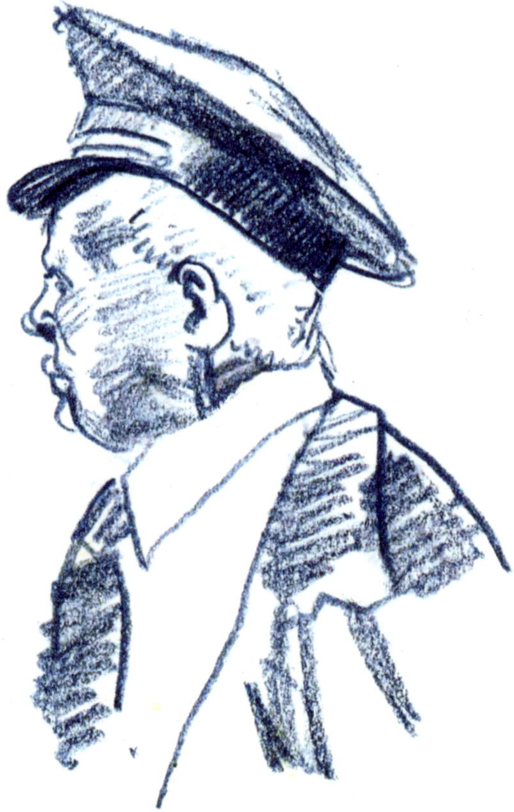

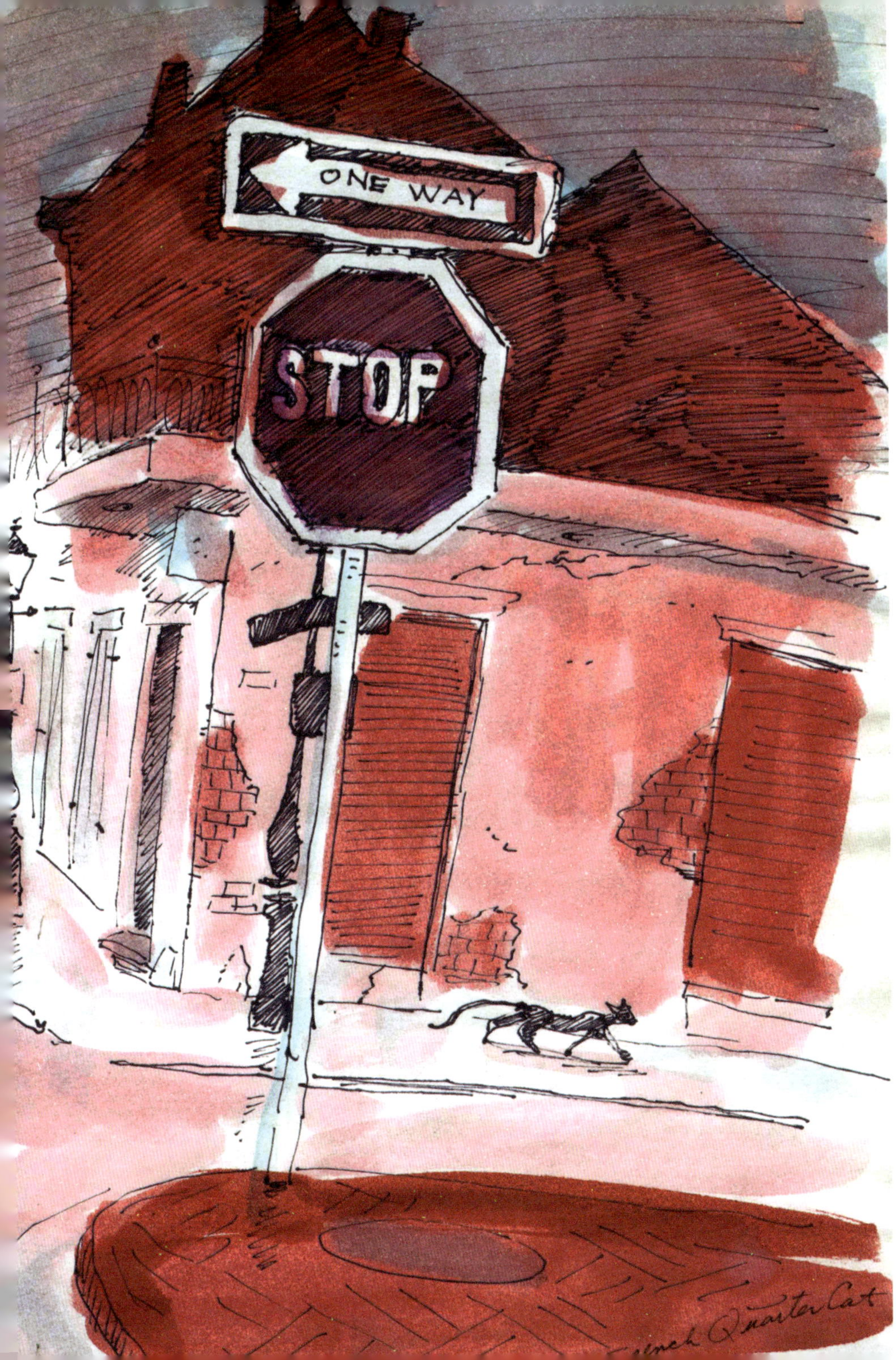
ONE WAY
STOP
Quarter Cat

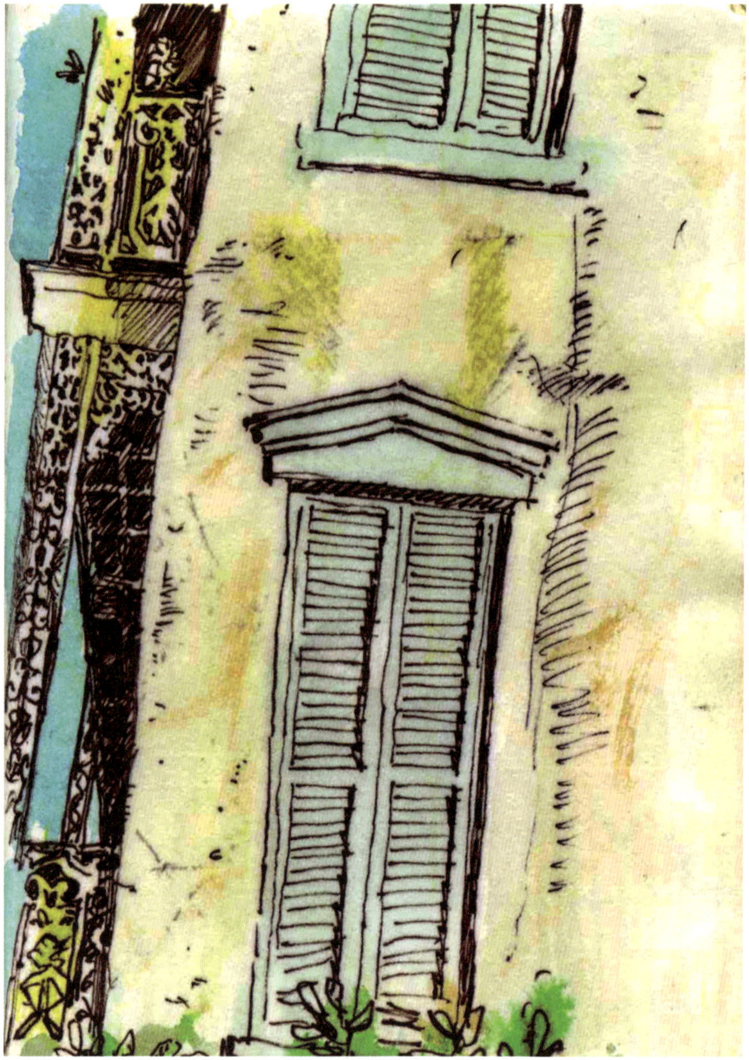

Somewhere down this street someone is playing *Saint James Infirmary* on a trumpet.

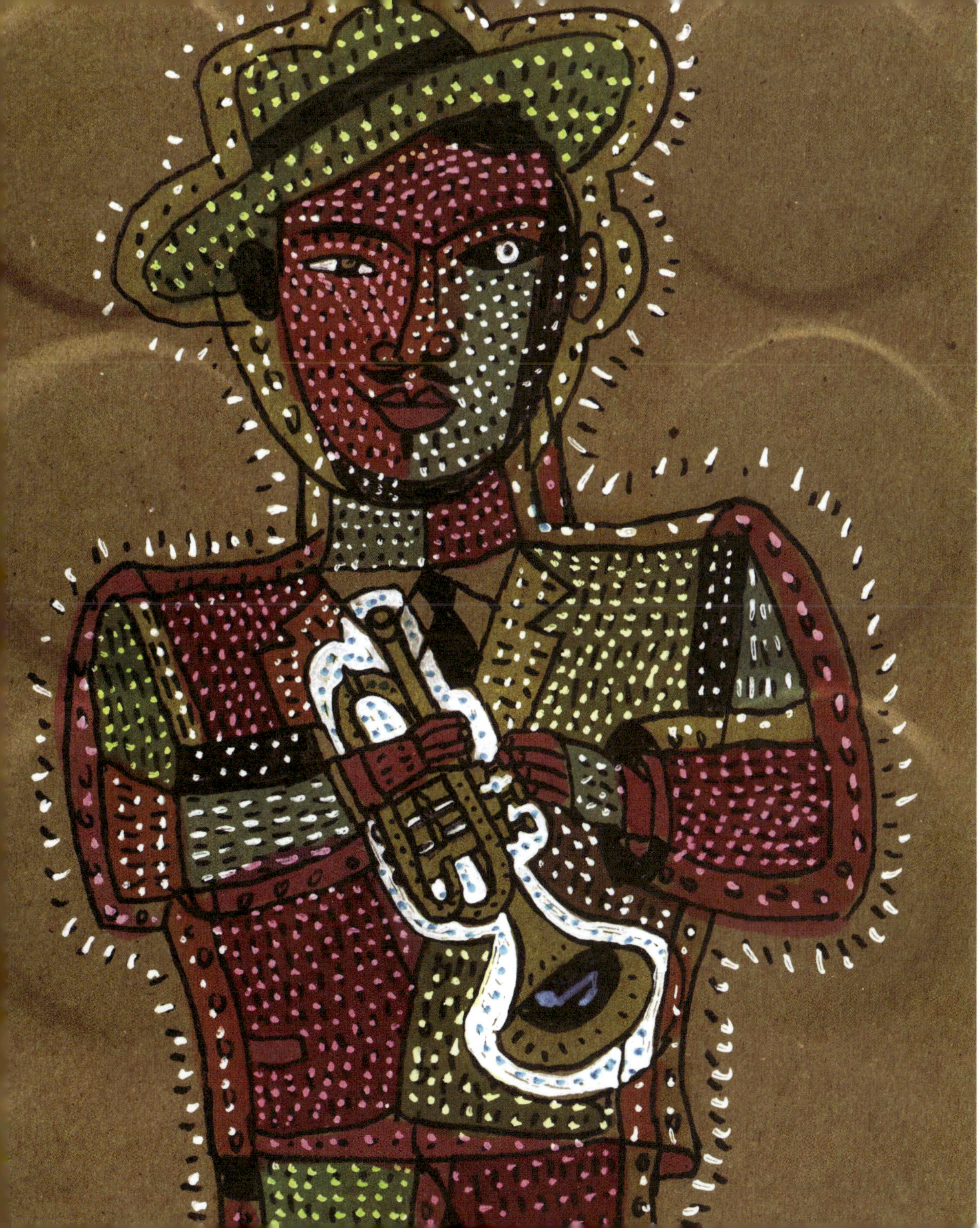

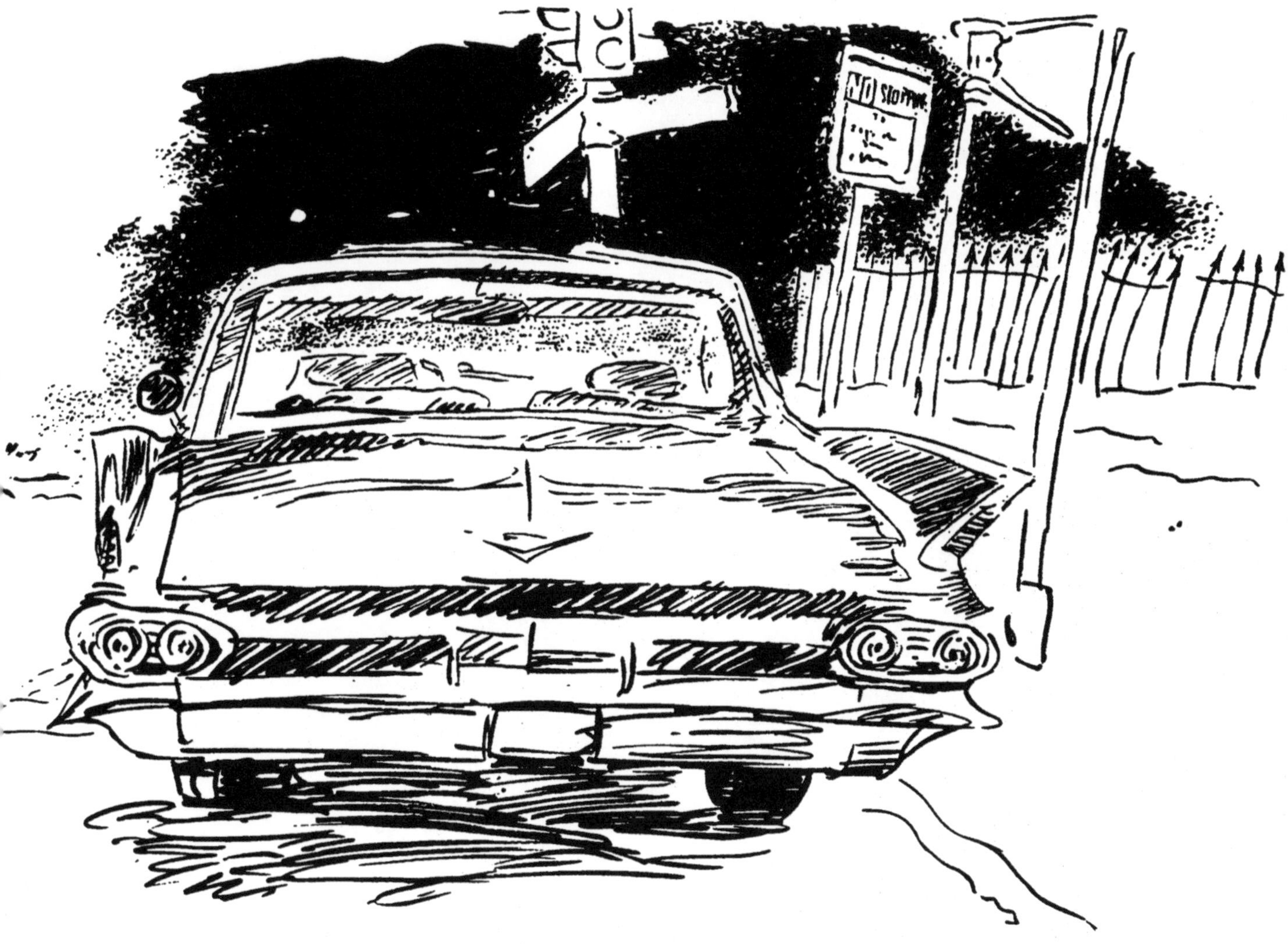


Big black Cadillac on the edge of the Quarter.

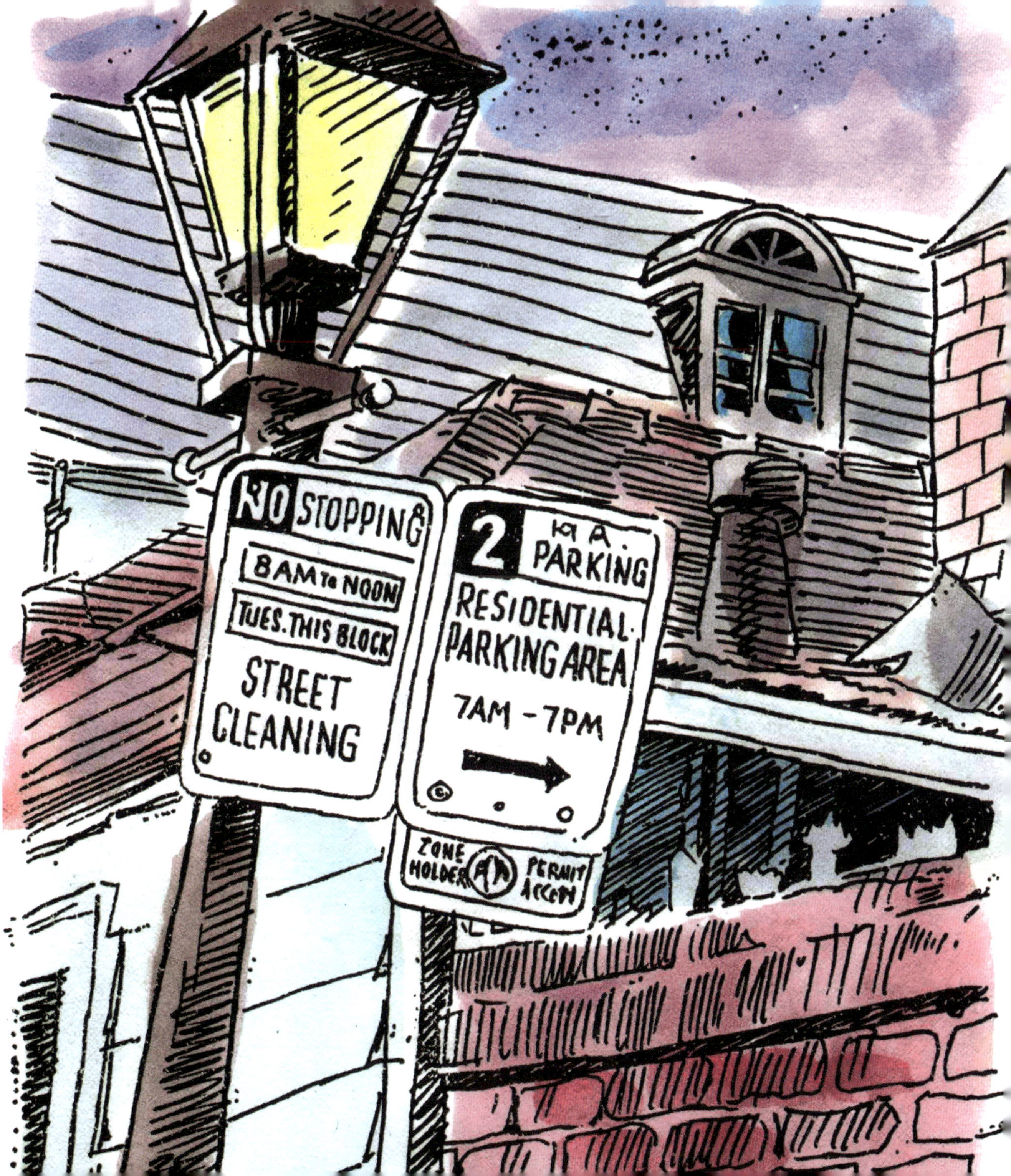
NO STOPPING
8AM to NOON
TUES. THIS BLOCK
STREET CLEANING
2
PARKING
RESIDENTIAL PARKING AREA
7AM - 7PM
ZONE HOLDER
PERMIT

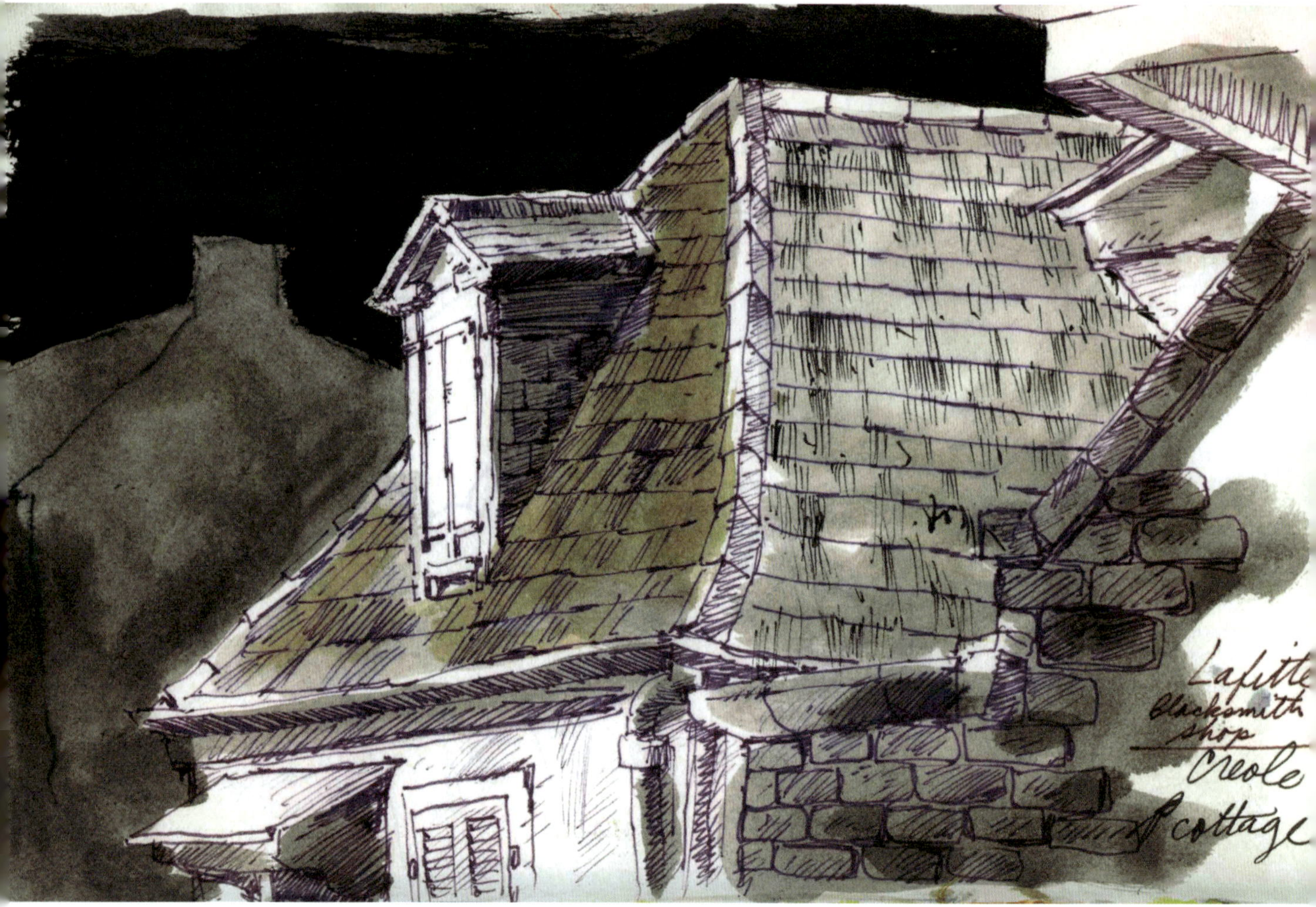


Old blacksmith shop of the pirate Jean Lafitte, one of the oldest Creole cottages left in the French Quarter.
In 1788 a fire destroyed most of New Orleans's French settlement of 800 buildings.
A second fire in 1794 took many of the remaining 200. The blacksmith shop survived it all.
Now it's a bar and it stays open all the time, come hell or high water.

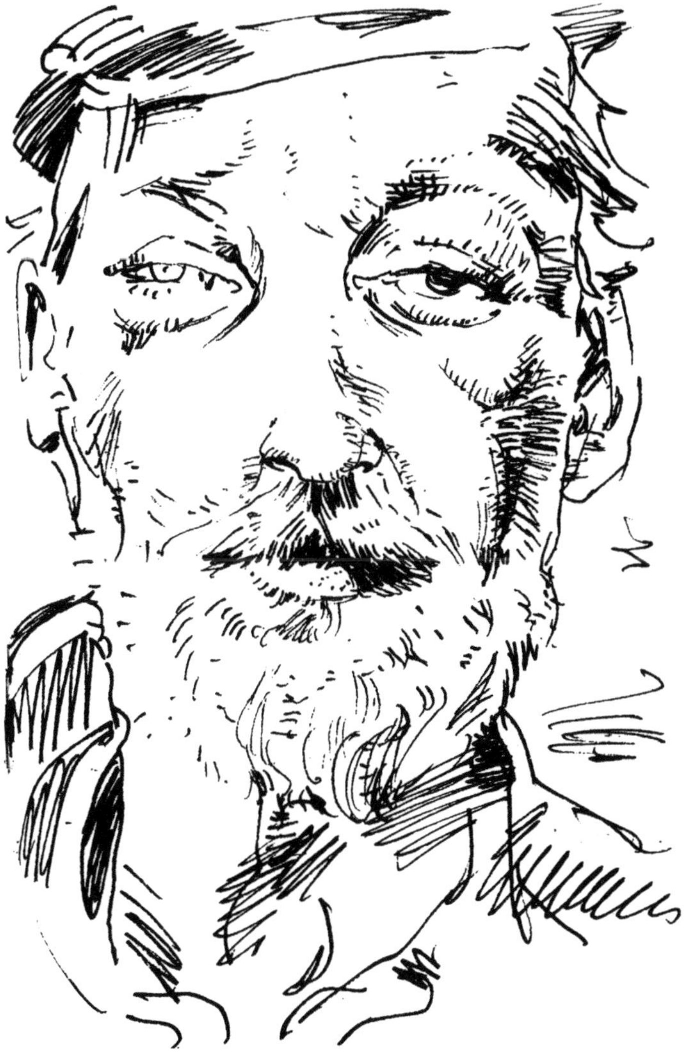

Homeless guy down by the river.

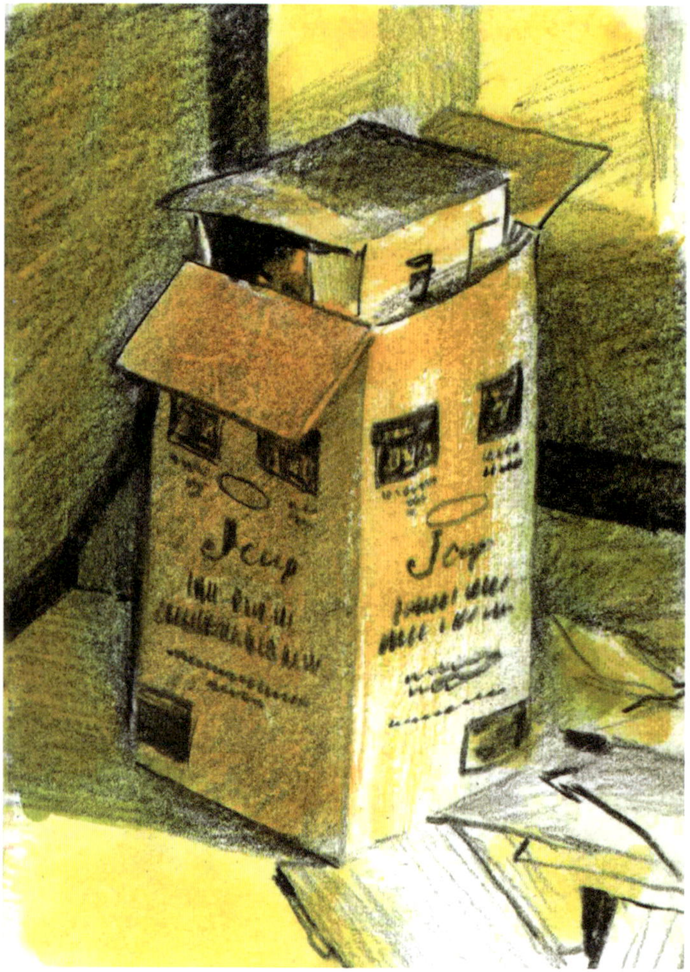




The sun has risen and the light streams down Wilkenson Row.
A bunch of cardboard boxes move. It says "Joy" on the outside,
but inside is a homeless guy with his head poking out like a periscope.
I bought him a cup of coffee around the corner at La Marquise Pastry Shop.

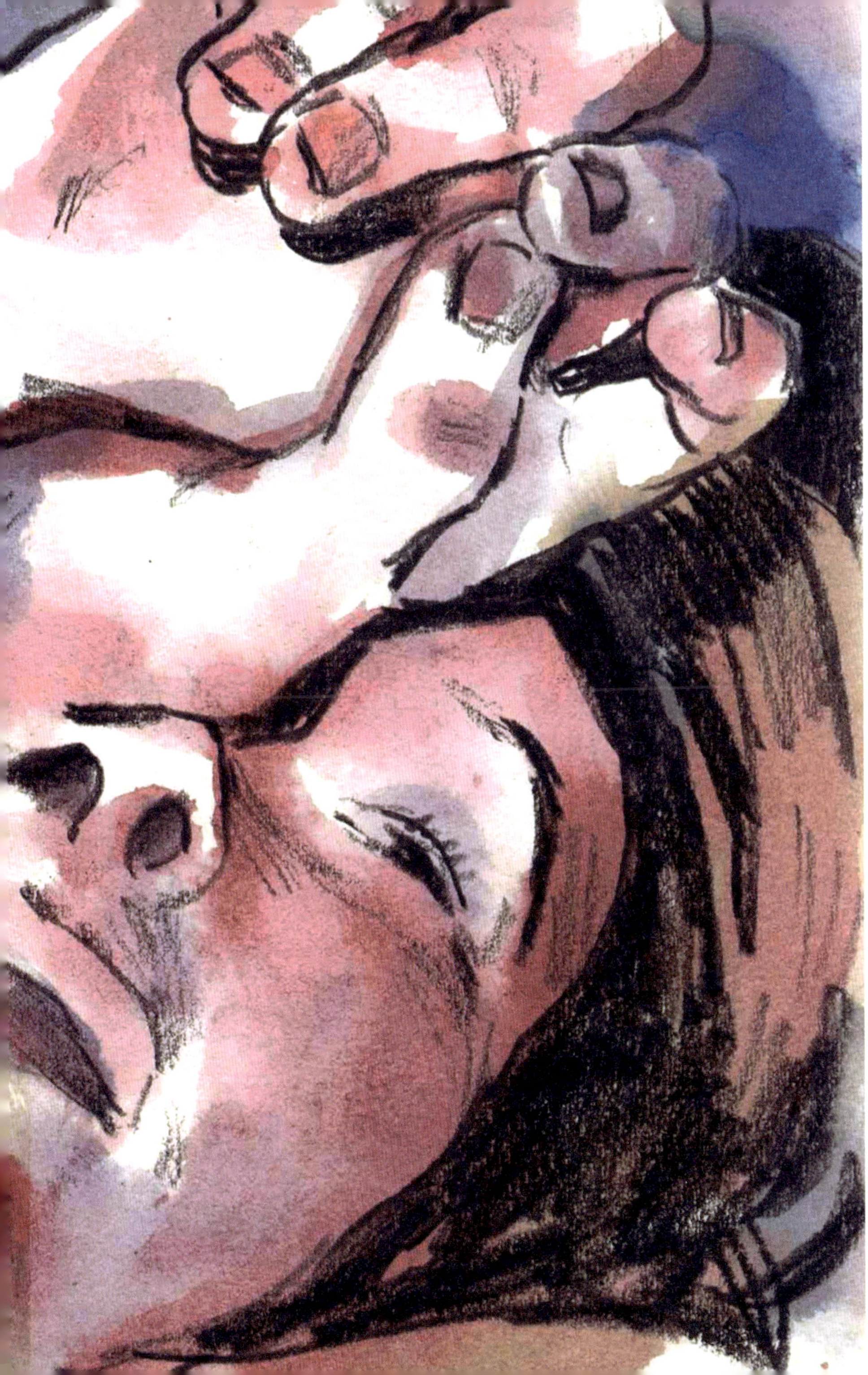

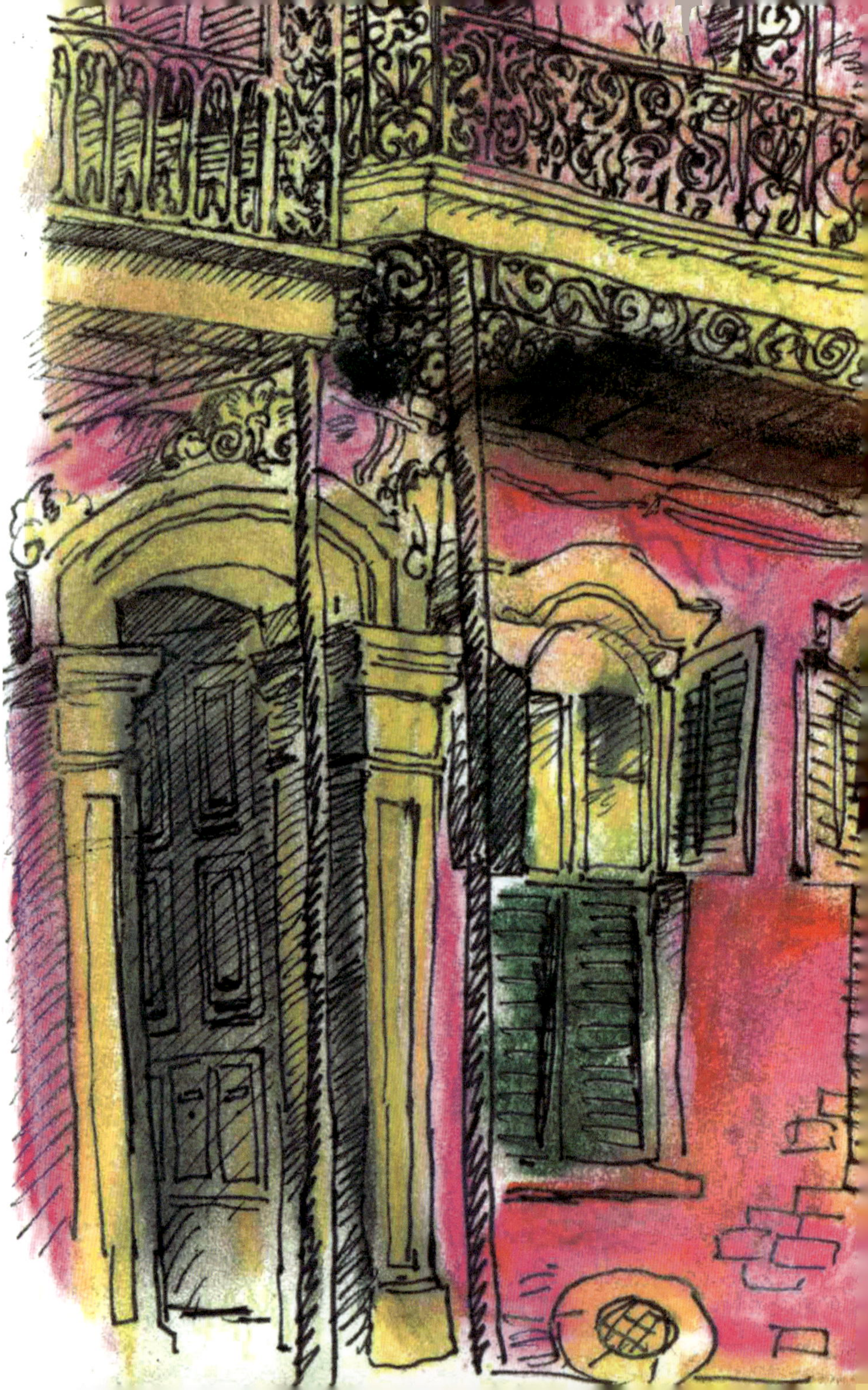

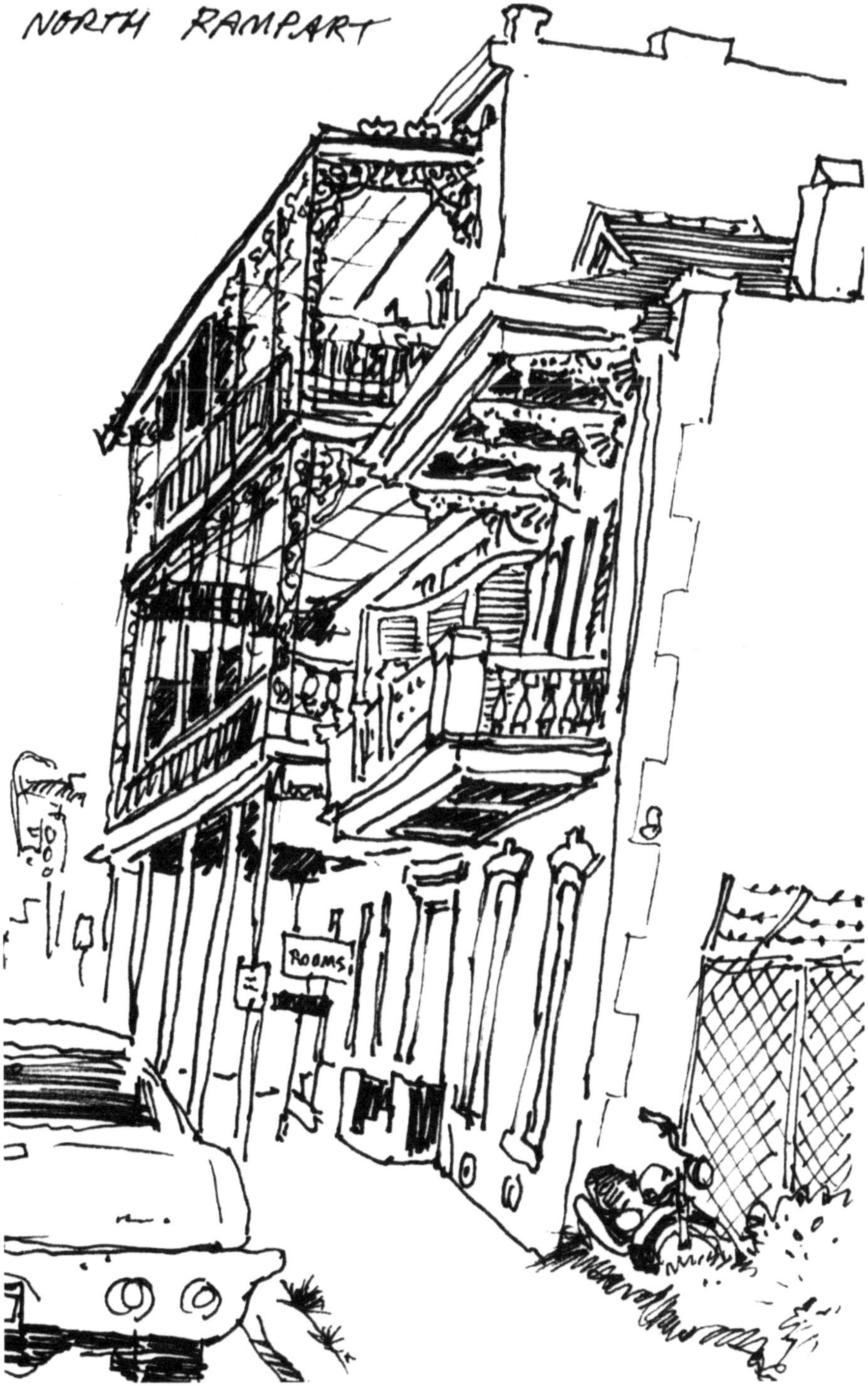
NORTH RAMPART
ROOMS

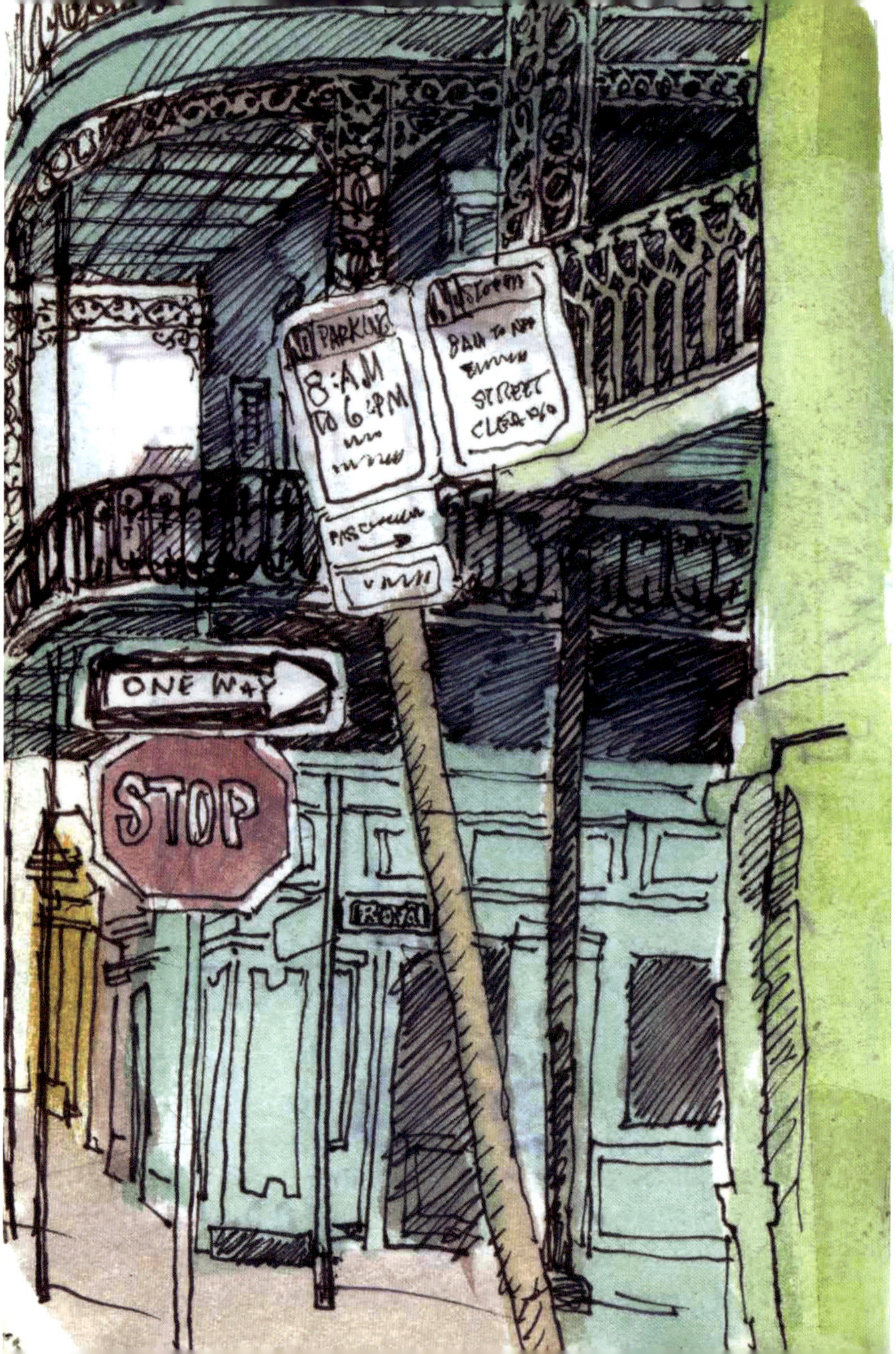
PARKING
8:AM
TO 6 PM
STREET
ONE WAY
STOP
Royal

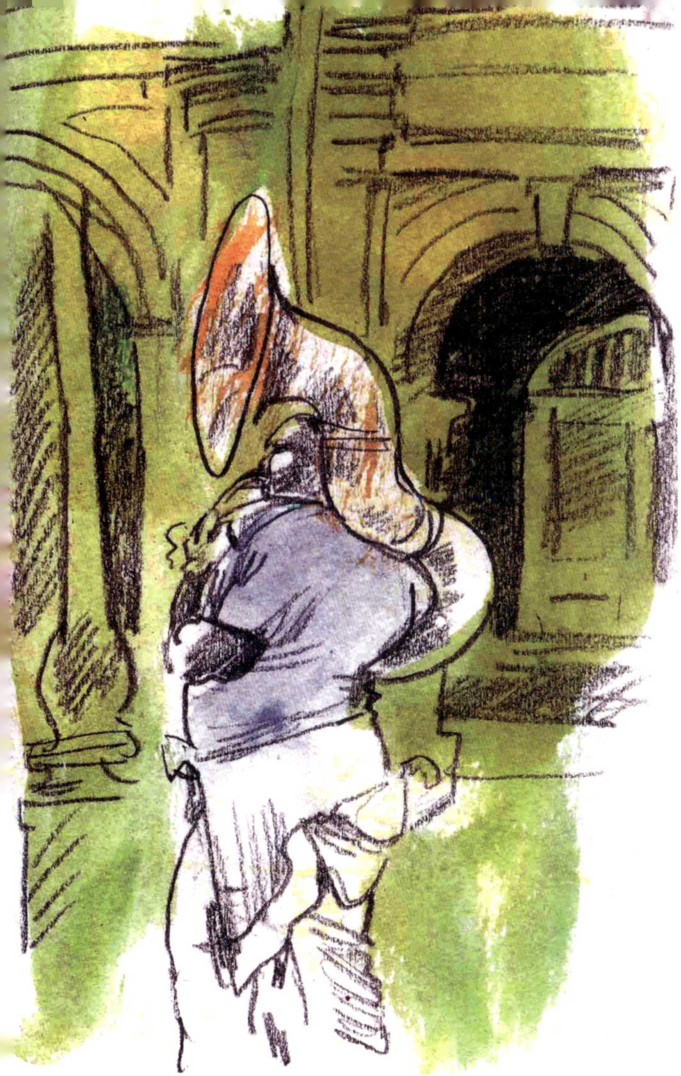

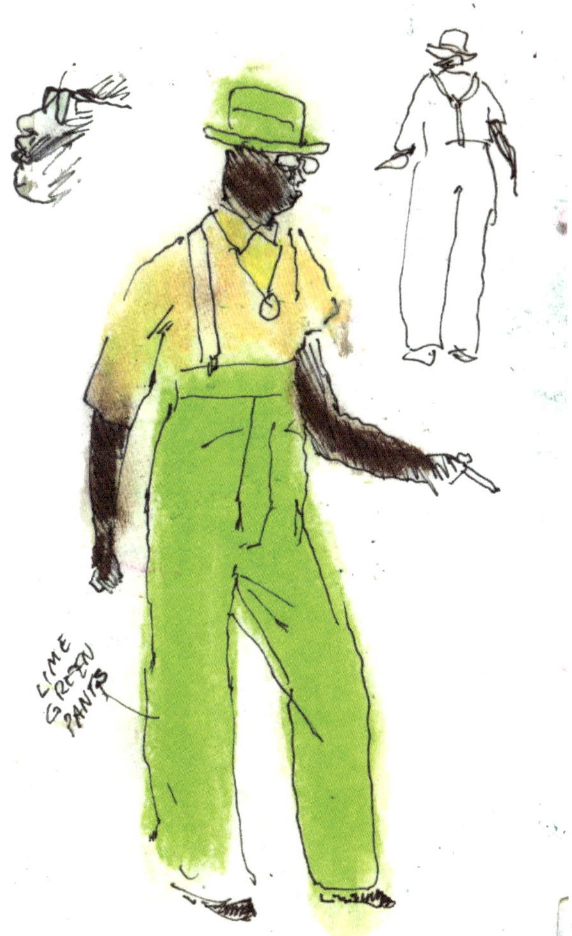


A slight fog disappears in Jackson Square as morning starts and New Orleans begins another day.
The tuba player waits for his companions. A gentleman in lime green pants is crossing in front of Saint Louis Cathedral on his way to Cafe du Monde for coffee and beignets.
It's already 90 degrees in the shade.

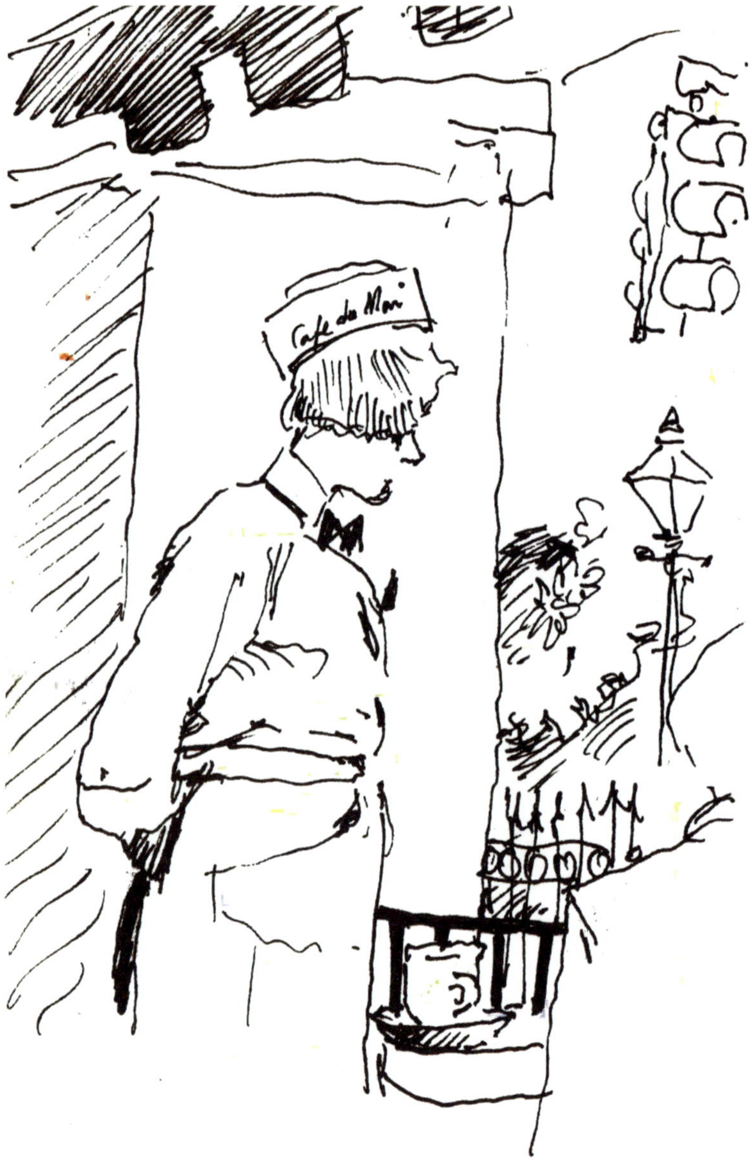

Cafe du Monde.

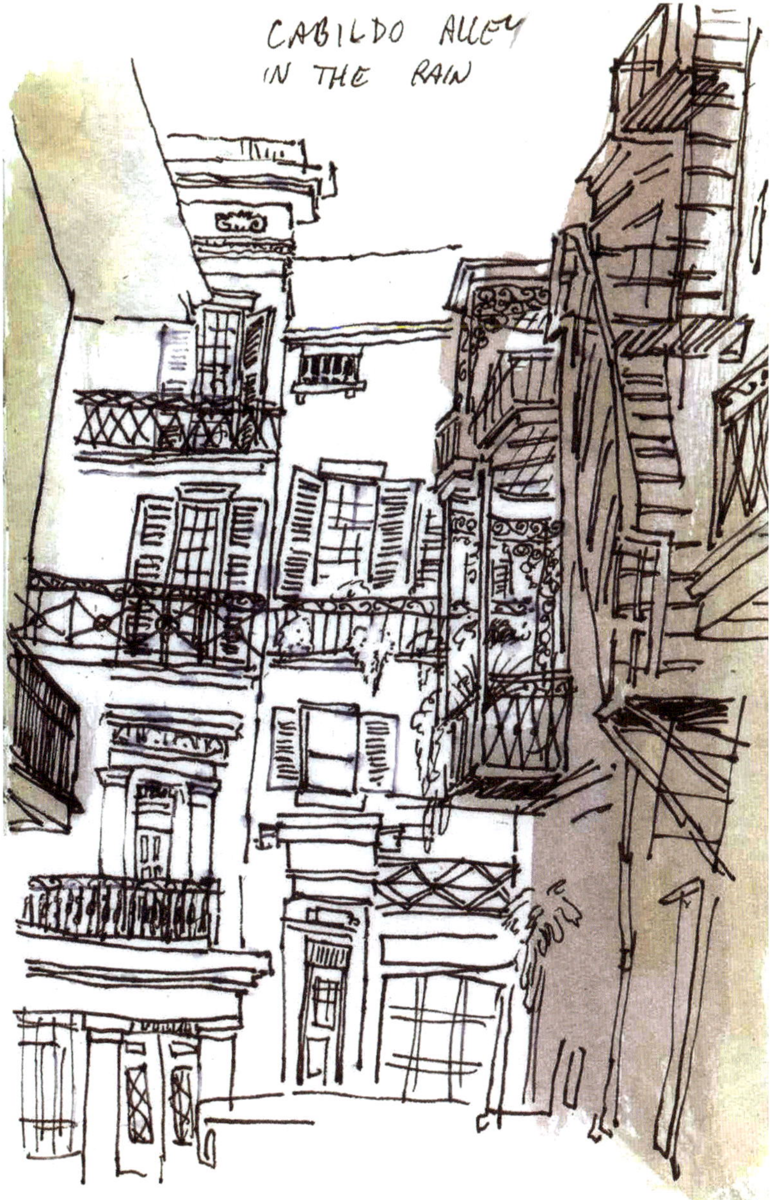
CABILDO ALLEY
IN THE RAIN

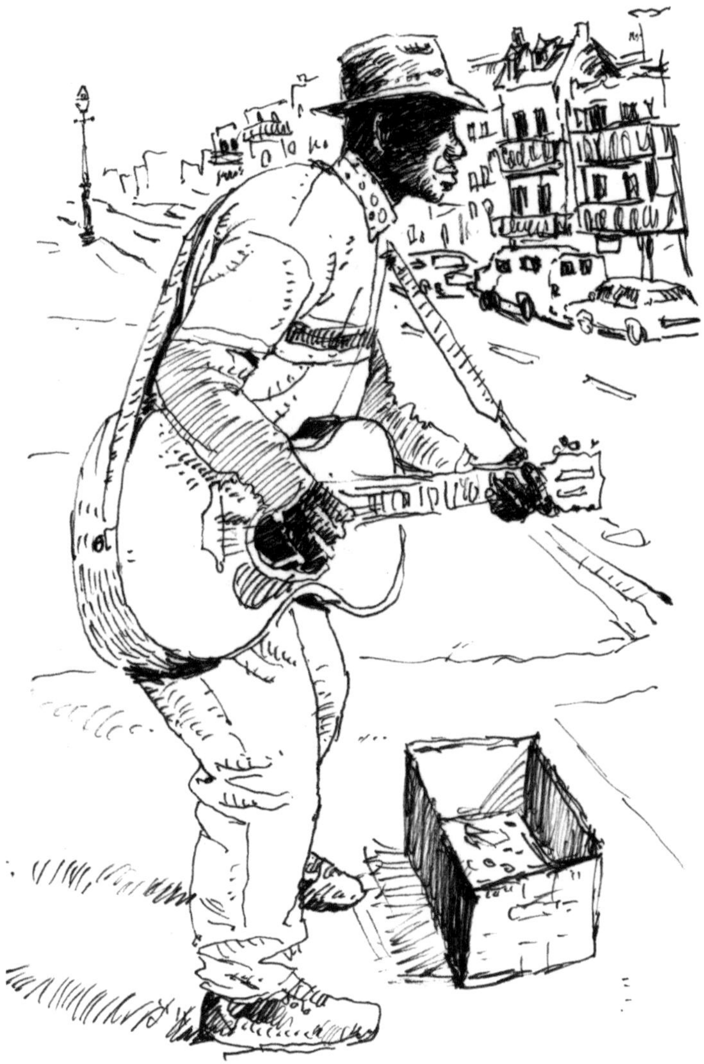

Blues man on Decatur Street.

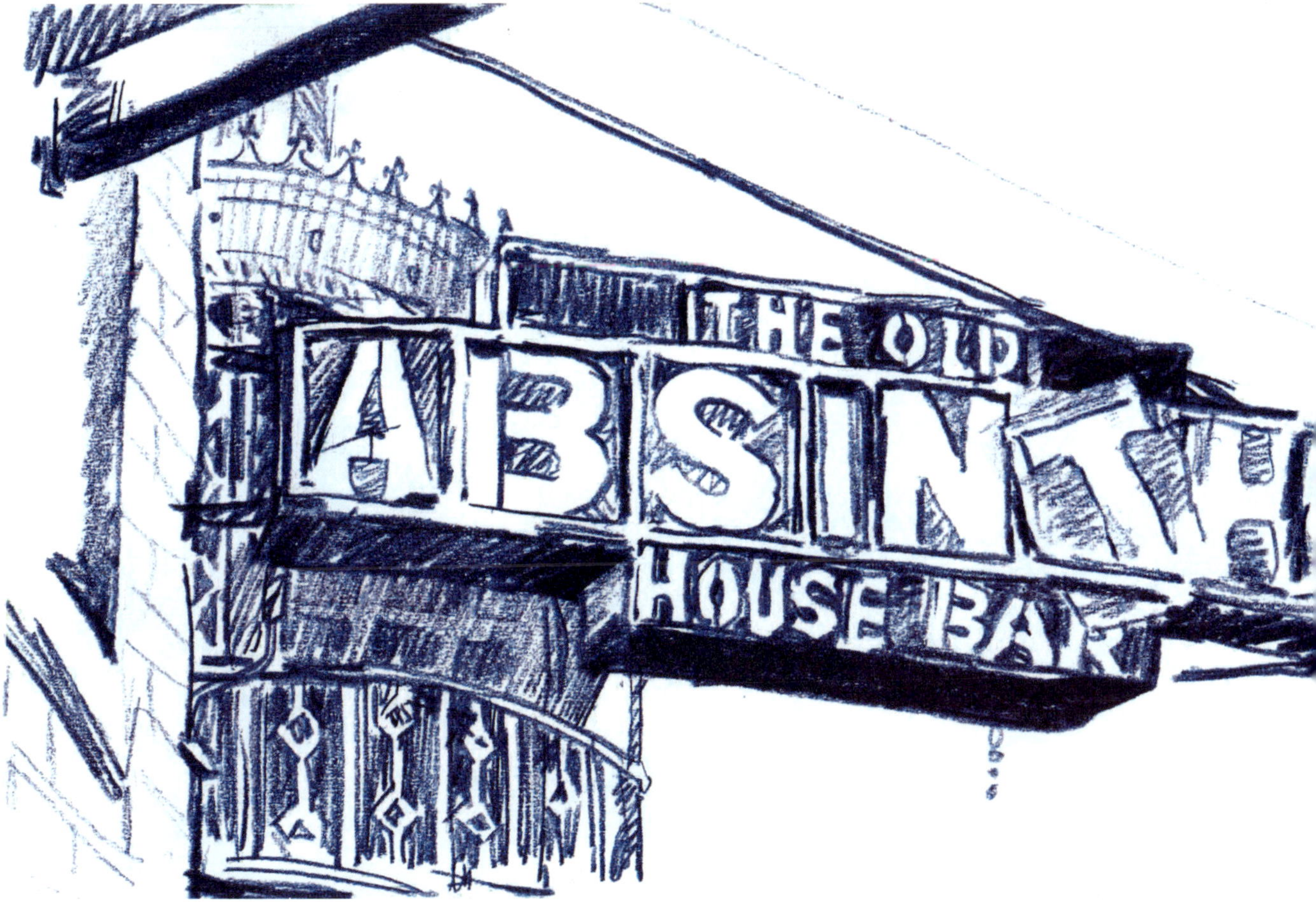




There was a time when the wicked and adventurous would come here to drink the drink of dreams: the Absinthe Frappe. But the Old Absinthe House on the corner of Bienville and Bourbon lost that reputation a long time ago. In its last incarnation it was a shiny new daiquiri shop. The sign remains as a symbol of a bygone era.

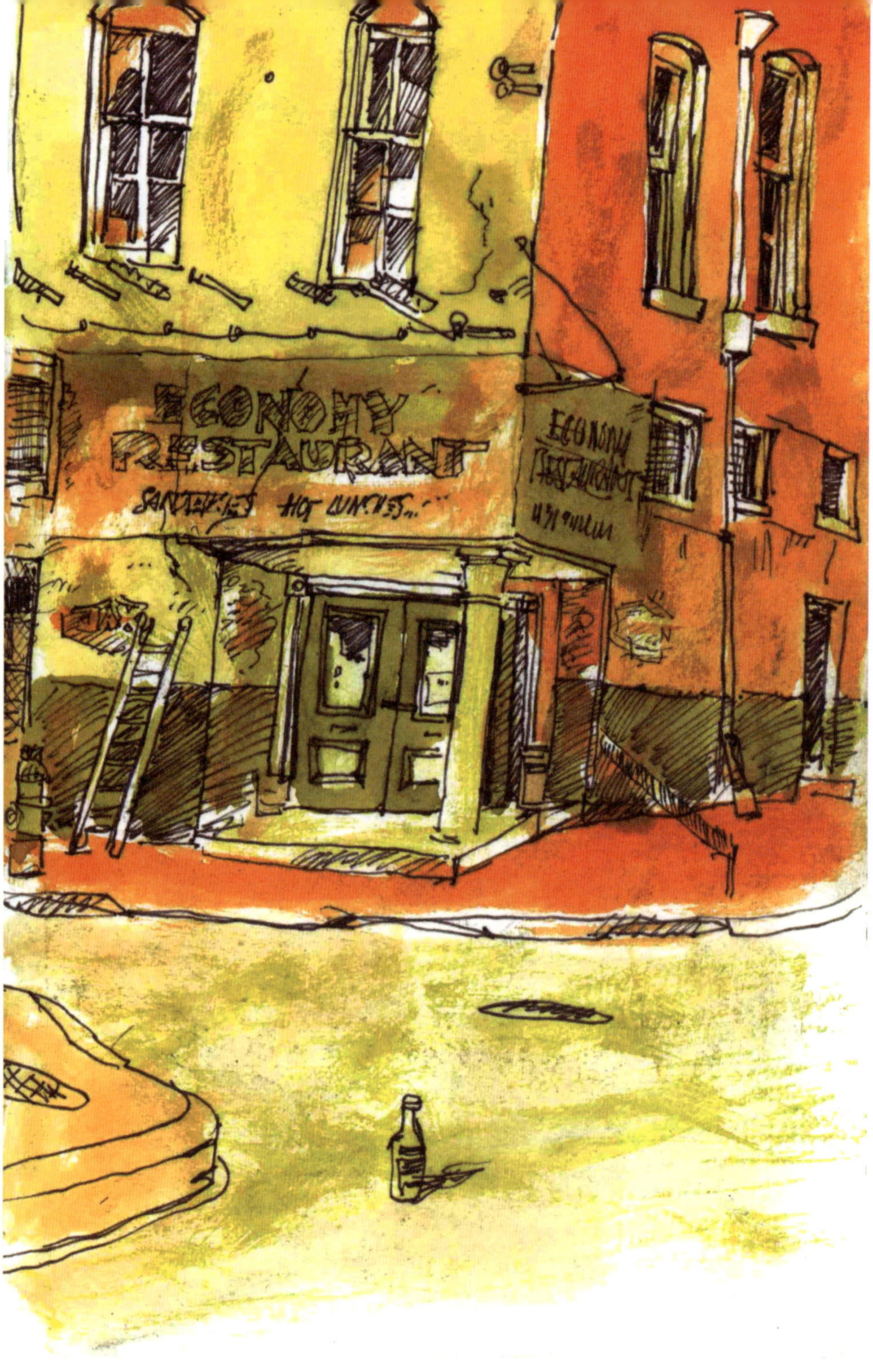
ECONOMY
RESTAURANT

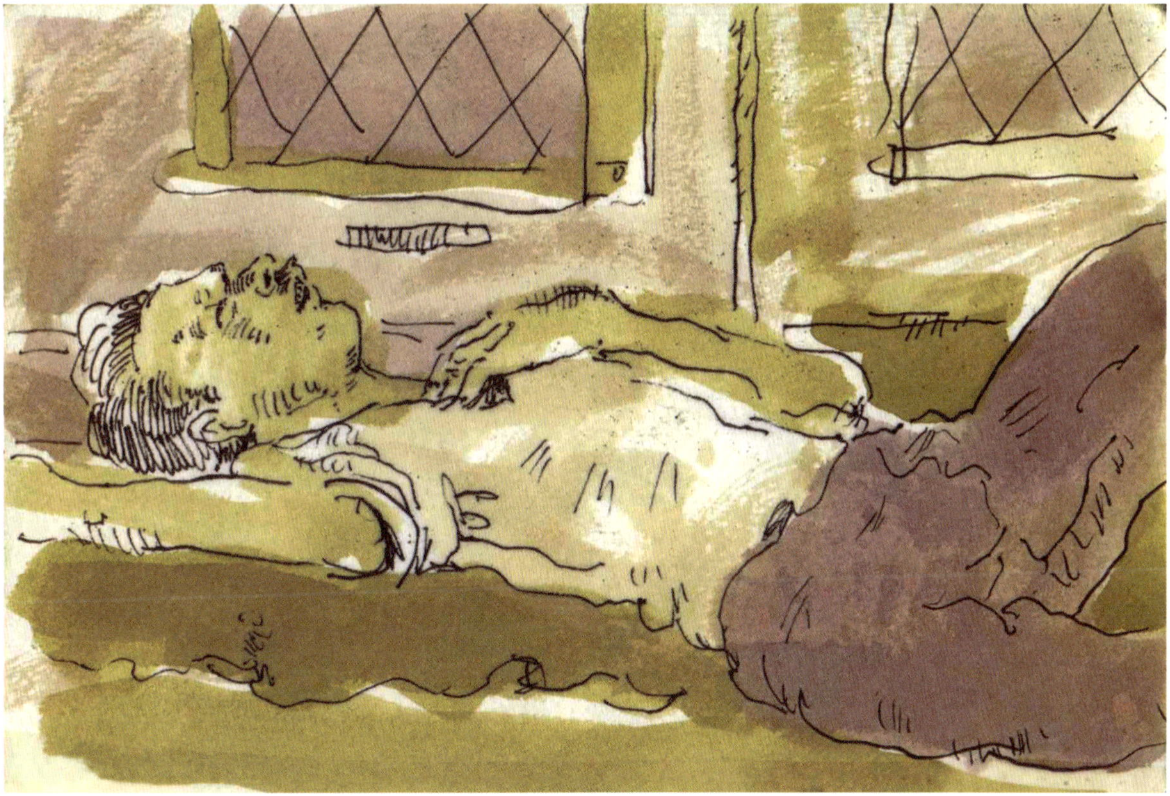



Bacchus, God of wine.

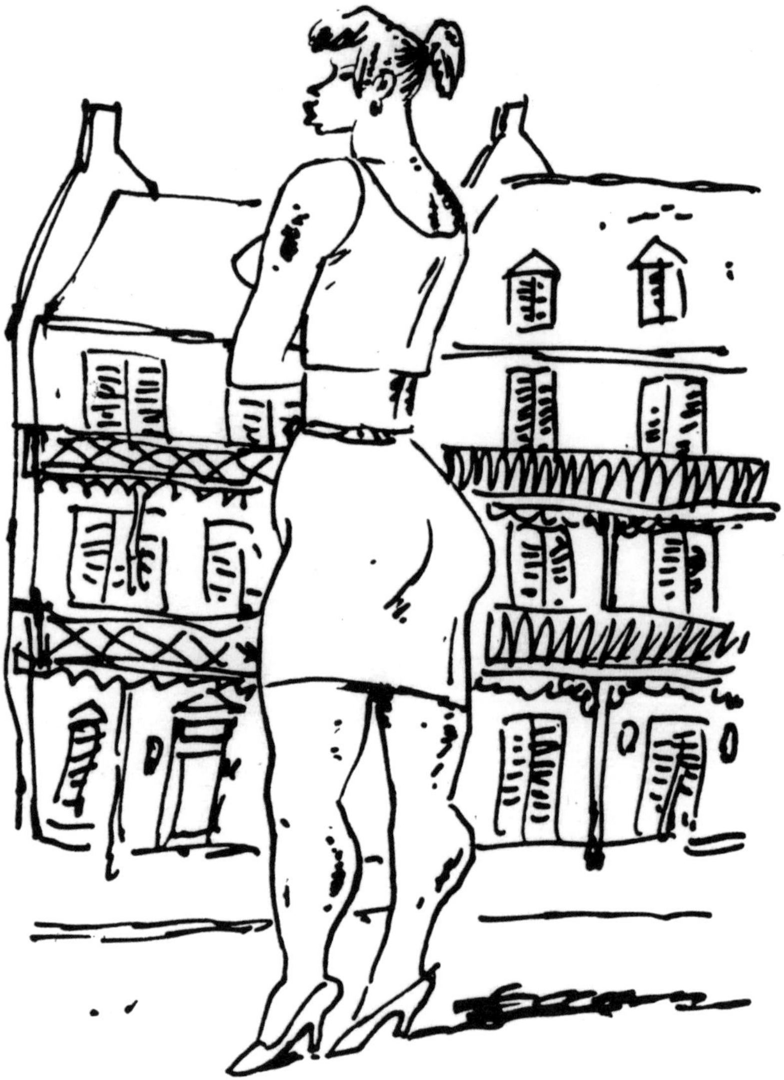

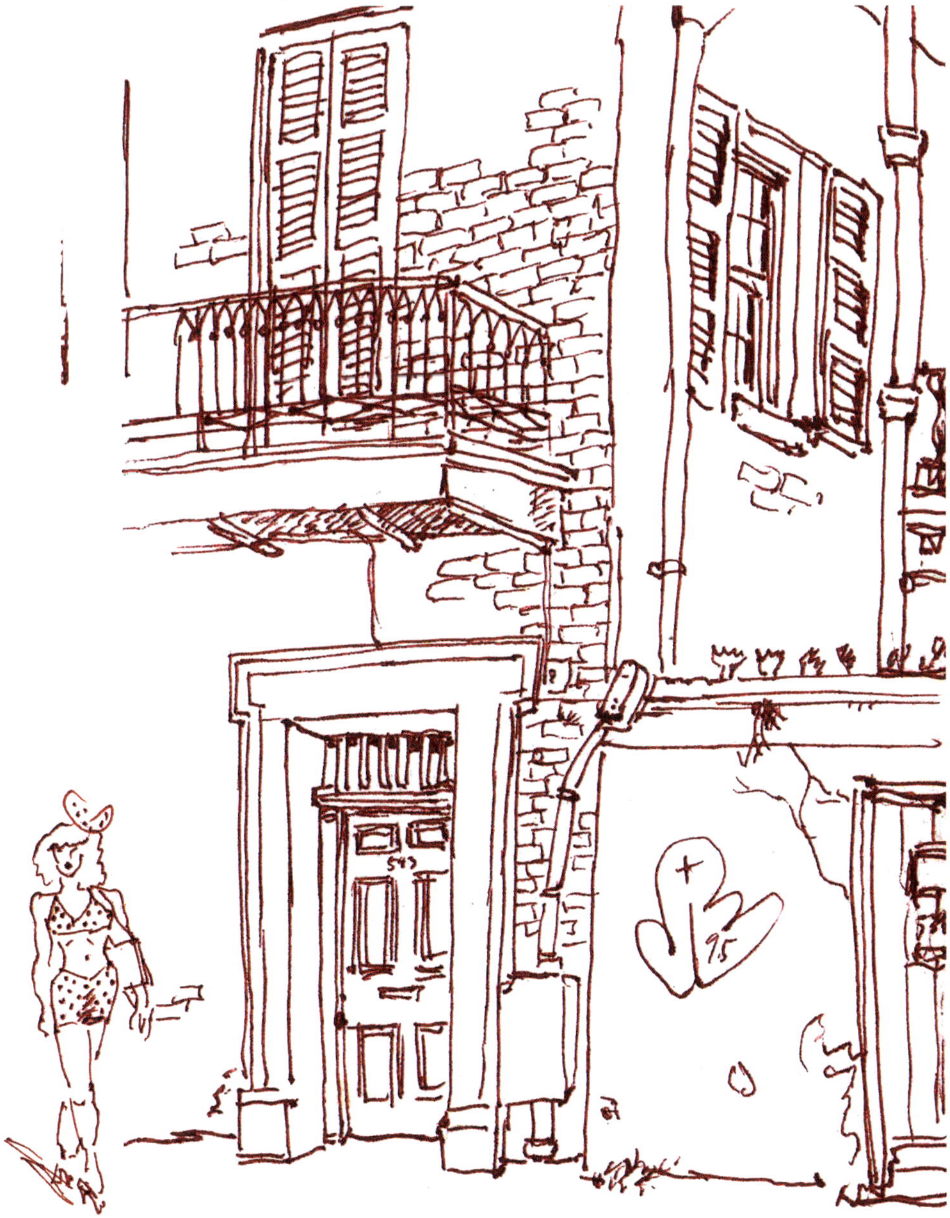

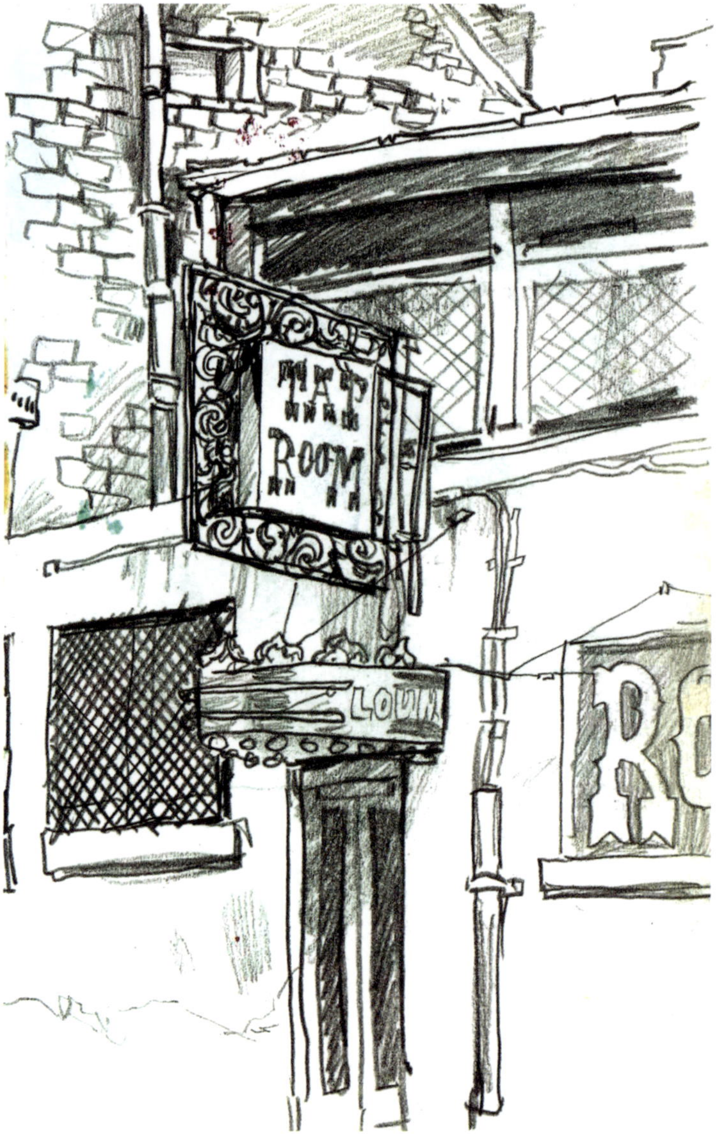
TAP
ROOM

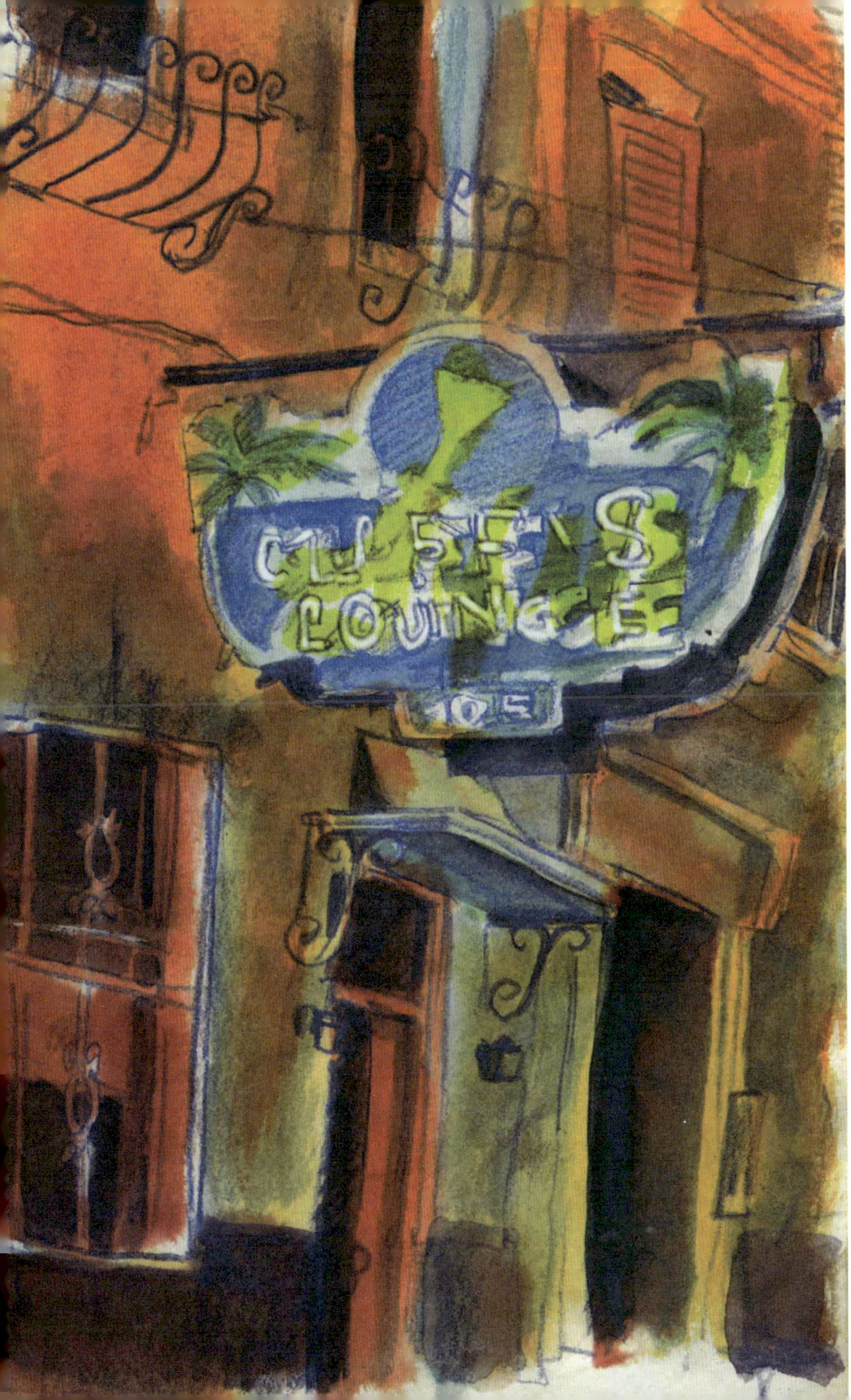
LOUNGE

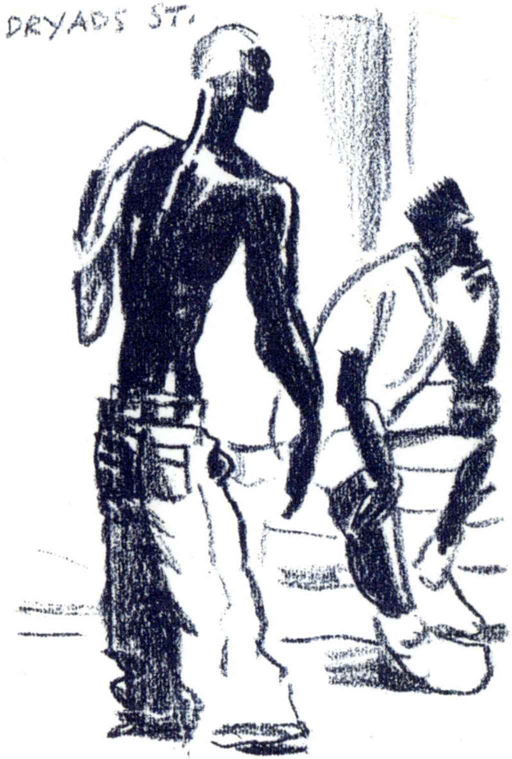
DRYADS ST.



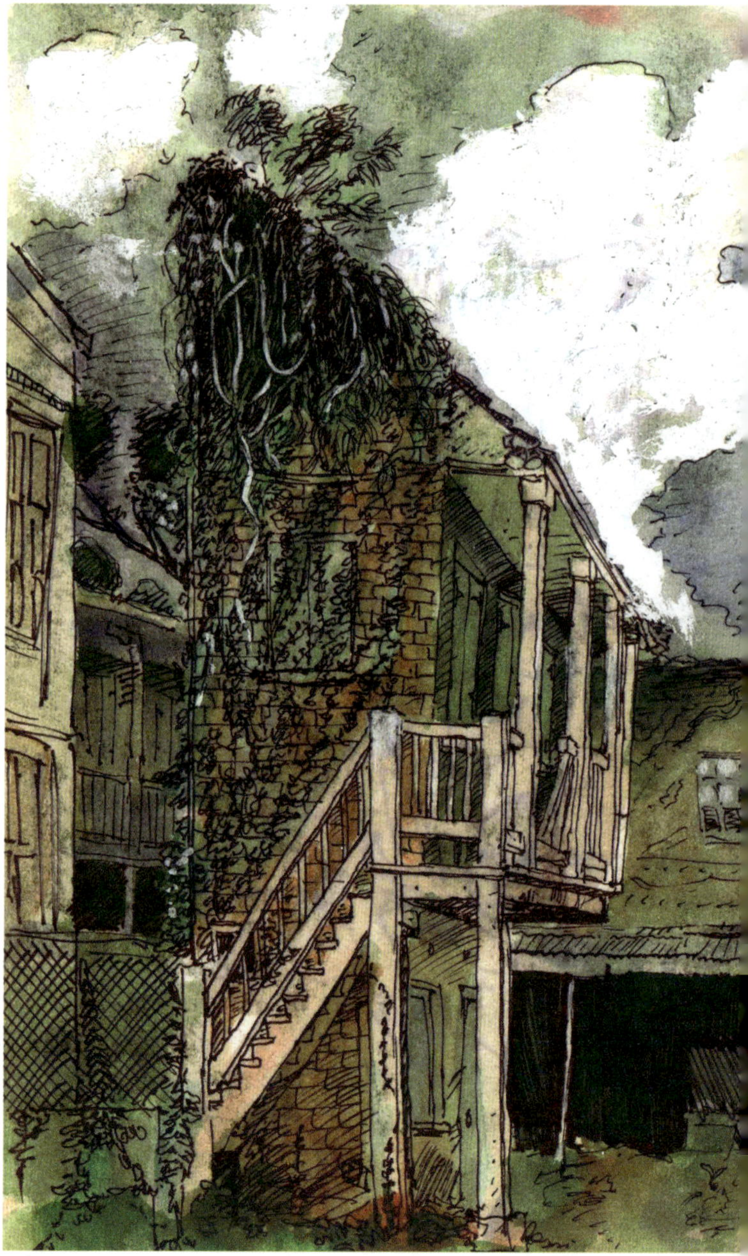

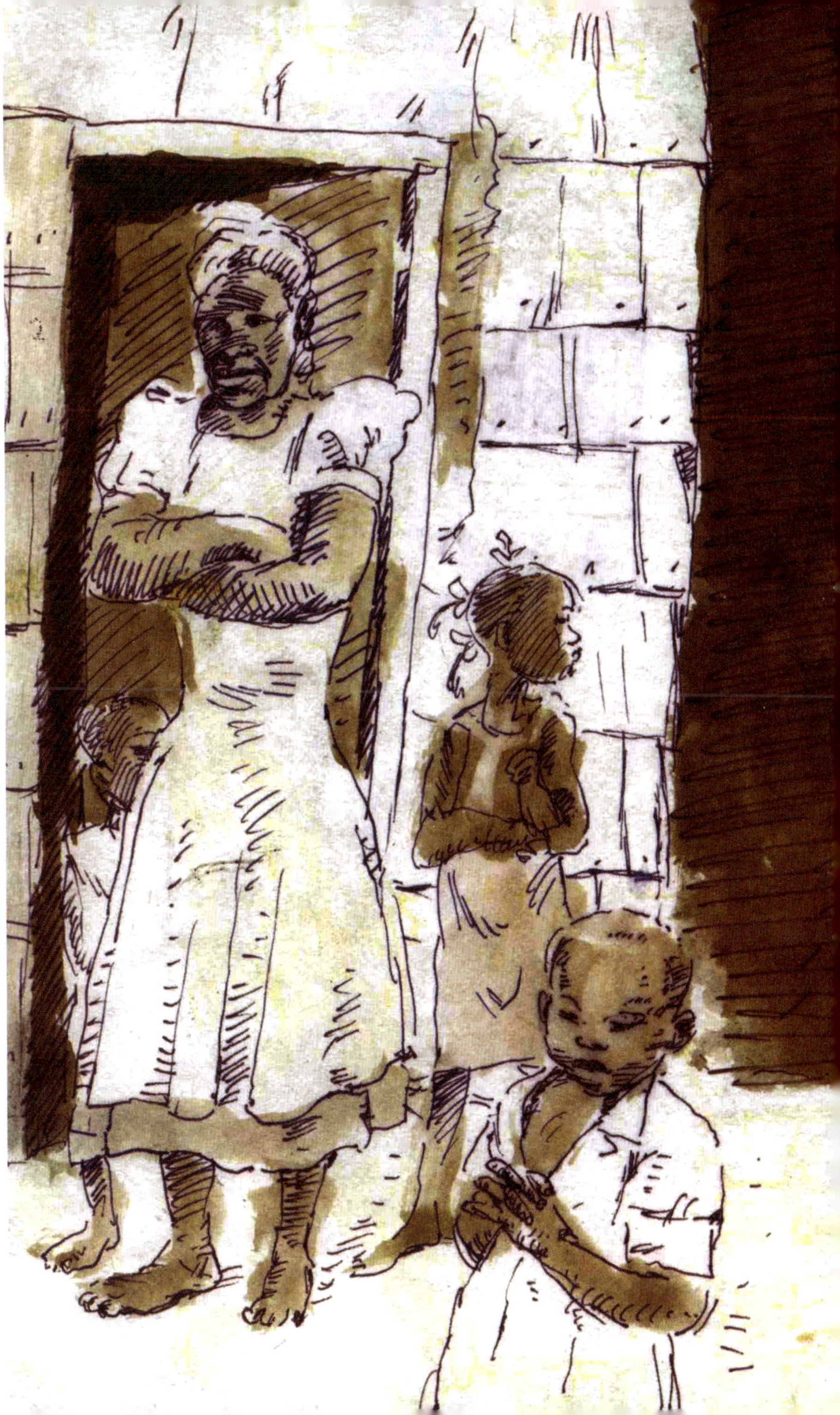

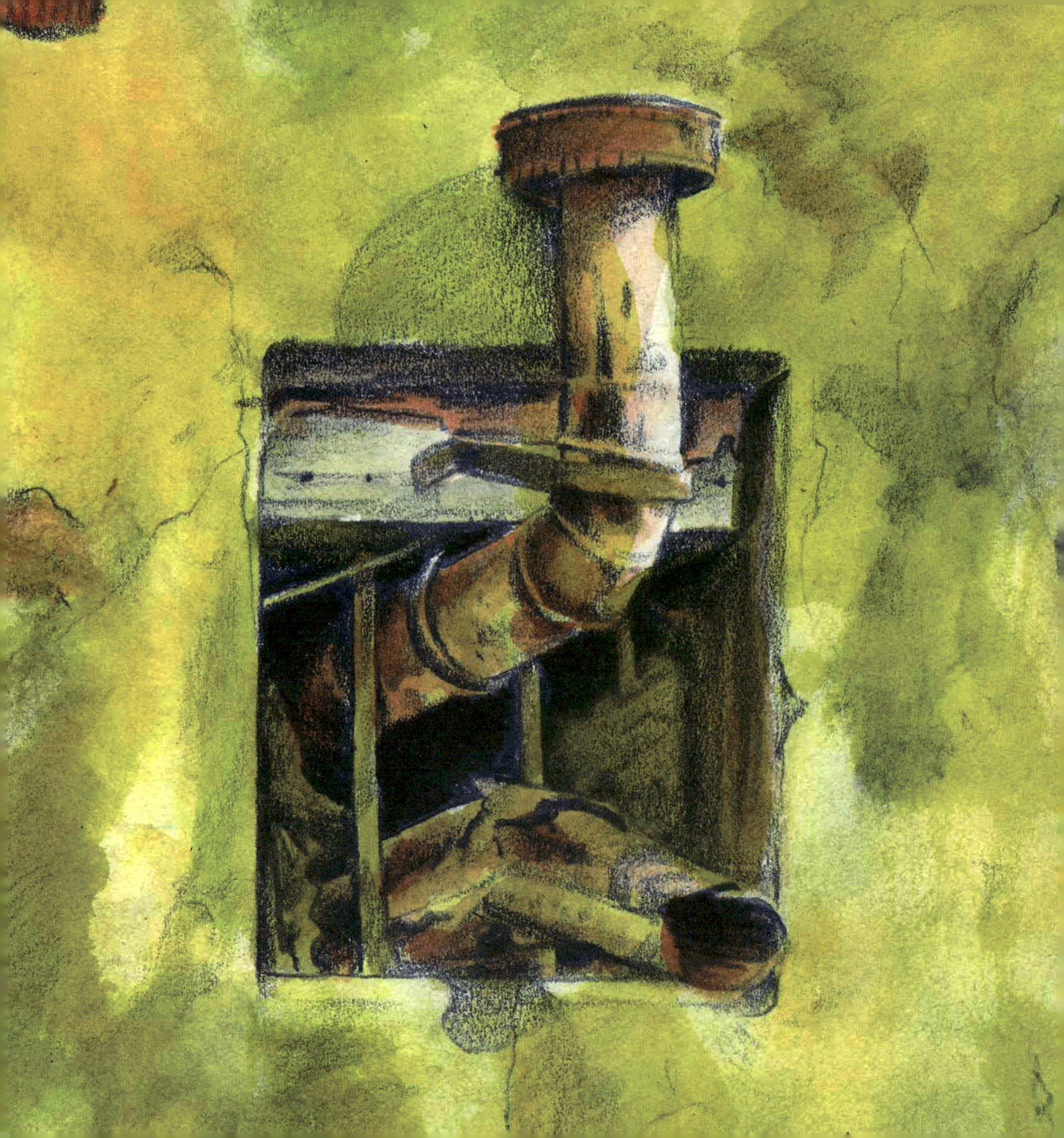

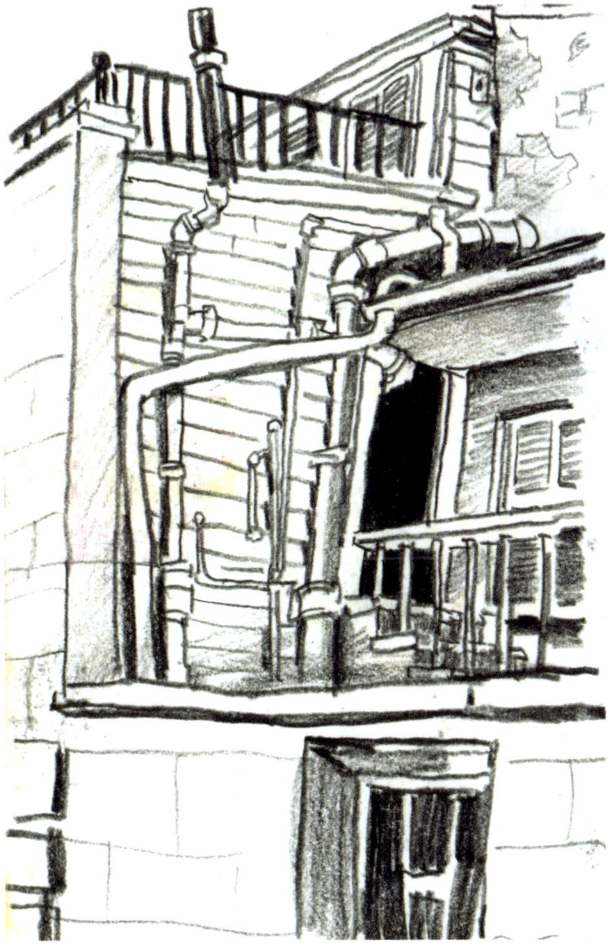



New Orleans plumbing and ventilation is a study in absurdly comedic execution. But it works nevertheless.

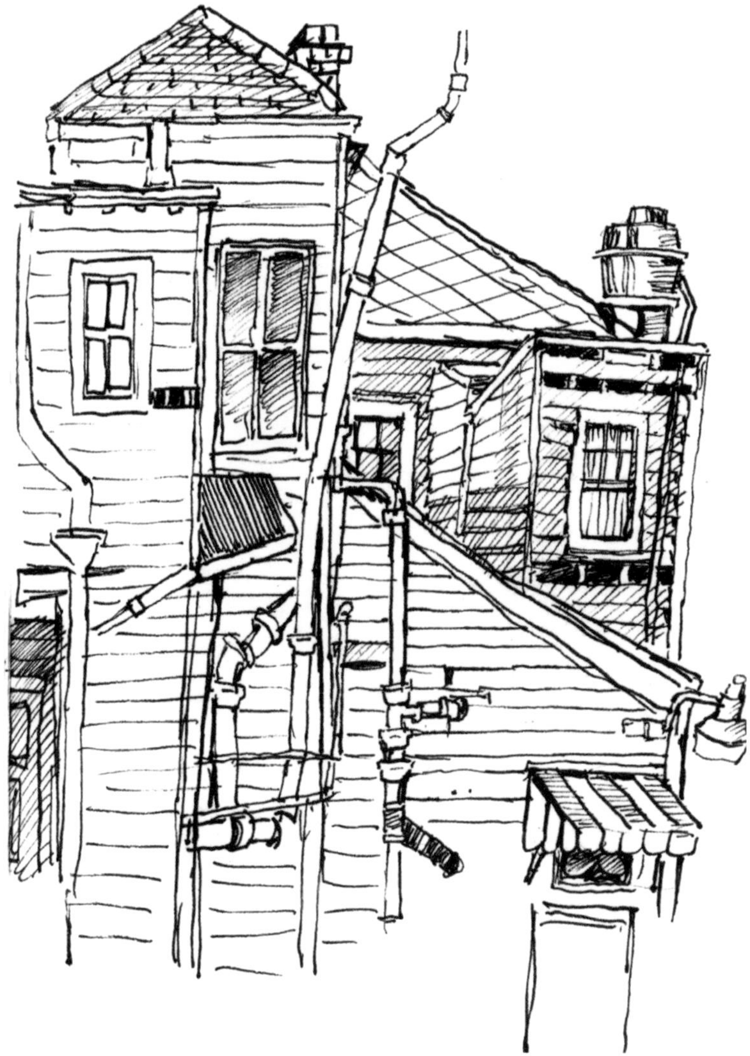

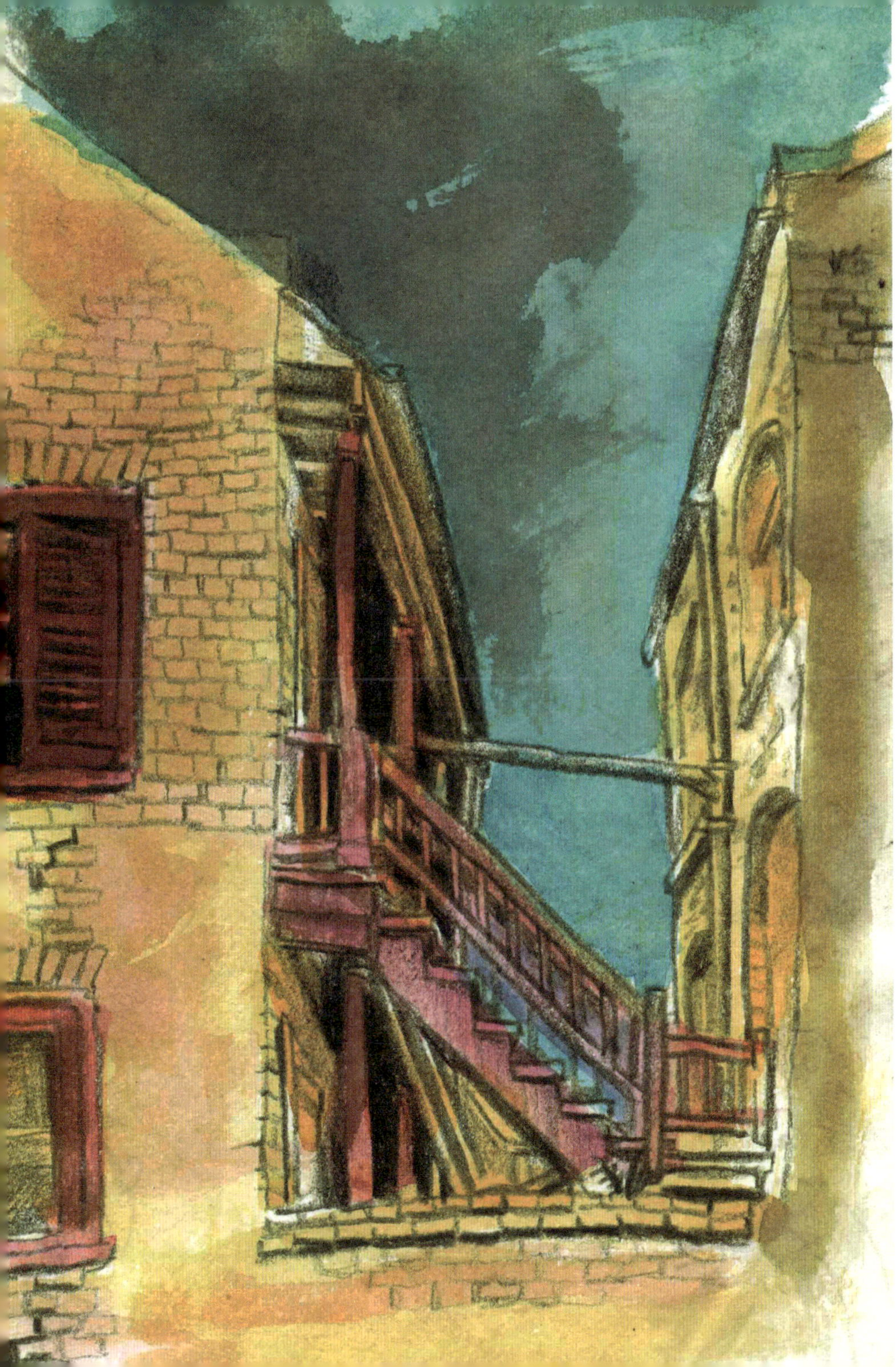

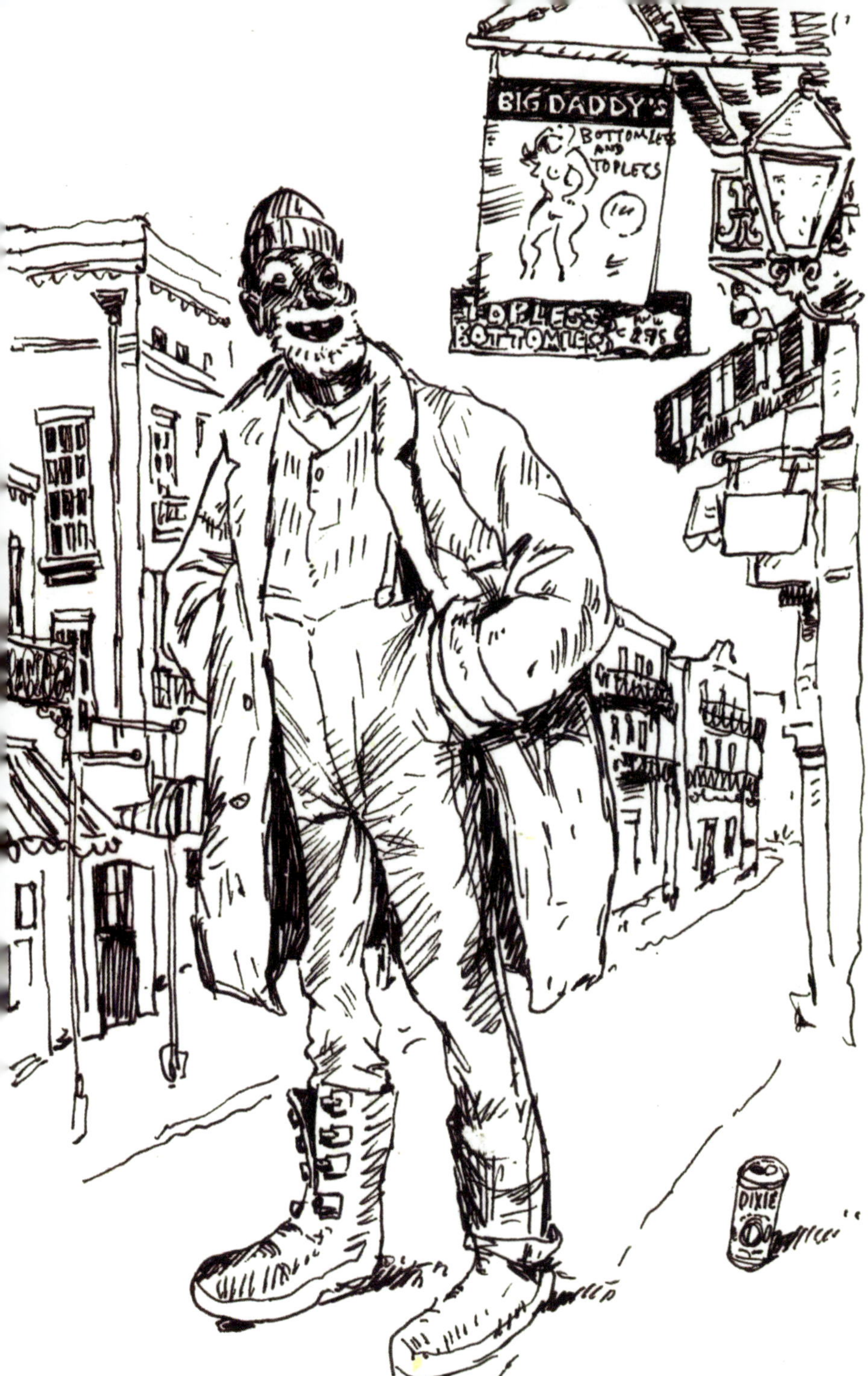
BIG DADDY'S
TOPLESS
DIXIE

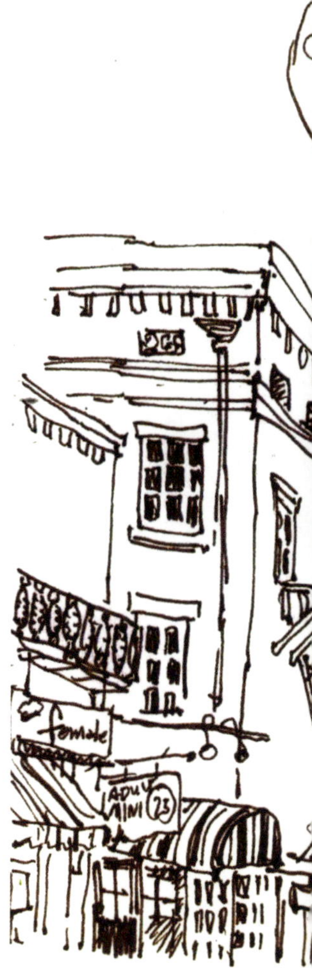
female
MINI
23

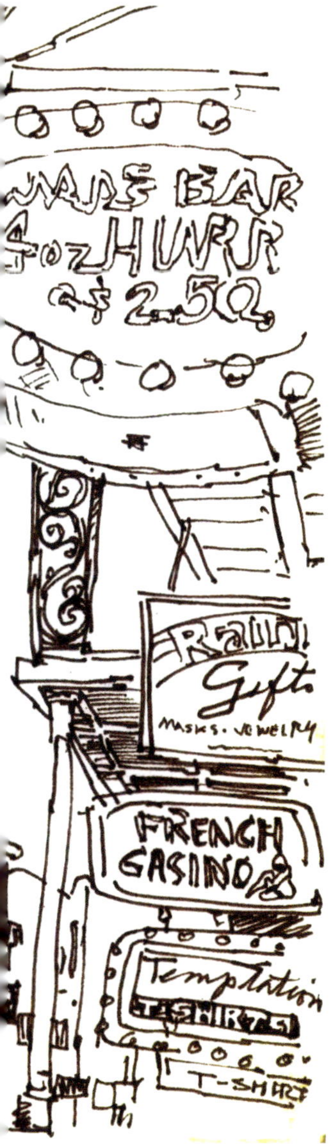


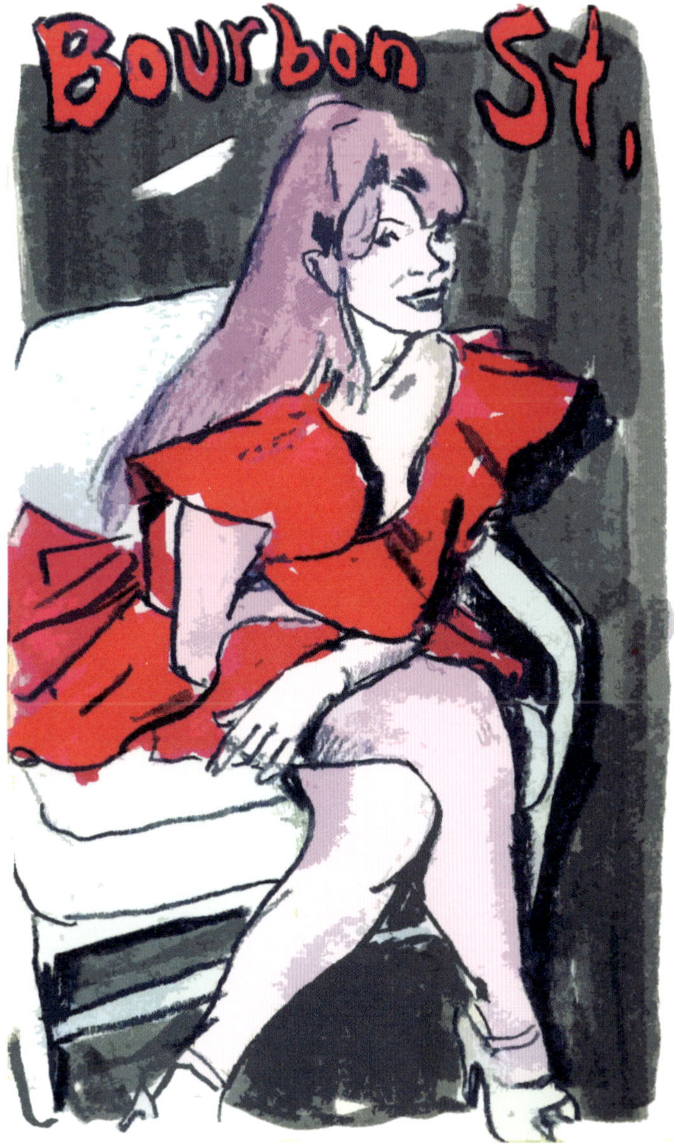


Bourbon Street.

WHILE SOME HAVE LABELED New Orleans as "Sin City," in truth it's a spiritual place. It was the birthplace of gospel great Mahalia Jackson. Her gravesite is about a mile from my home. I used to go there and leave bouquets of flowers on special holidays like Easter and Christmas.

If anyone could speak to God, it was Mahalia. Her music reached across predominantly racist America and inspired souls with her talent. The same was true of Louis Armstrong, who was also born in New Orleans.

Paula and I used to frequent the spiritualist churches in New Orleans' Ninth Ward. We didn't mind being the only white faces in the sea of believers. It was the most intensely spiritual music we ever heard, the root music of all blues and jazz.

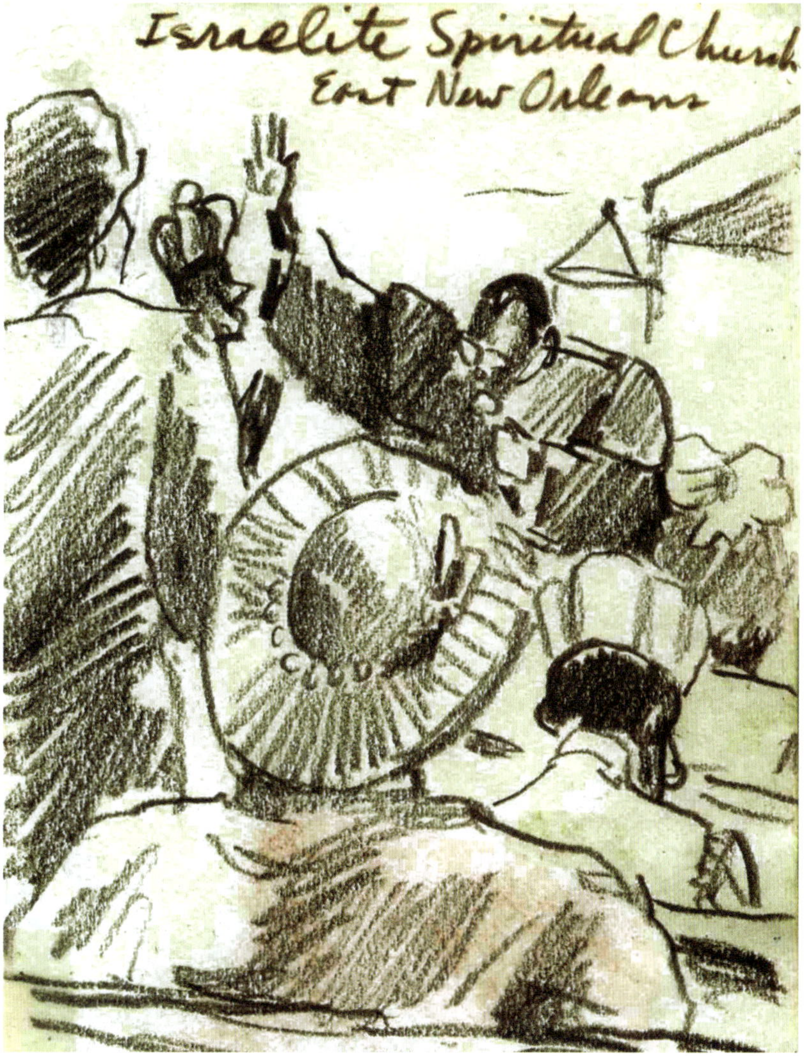


Ordination of bishops at a moment of Holy Ghost possession.

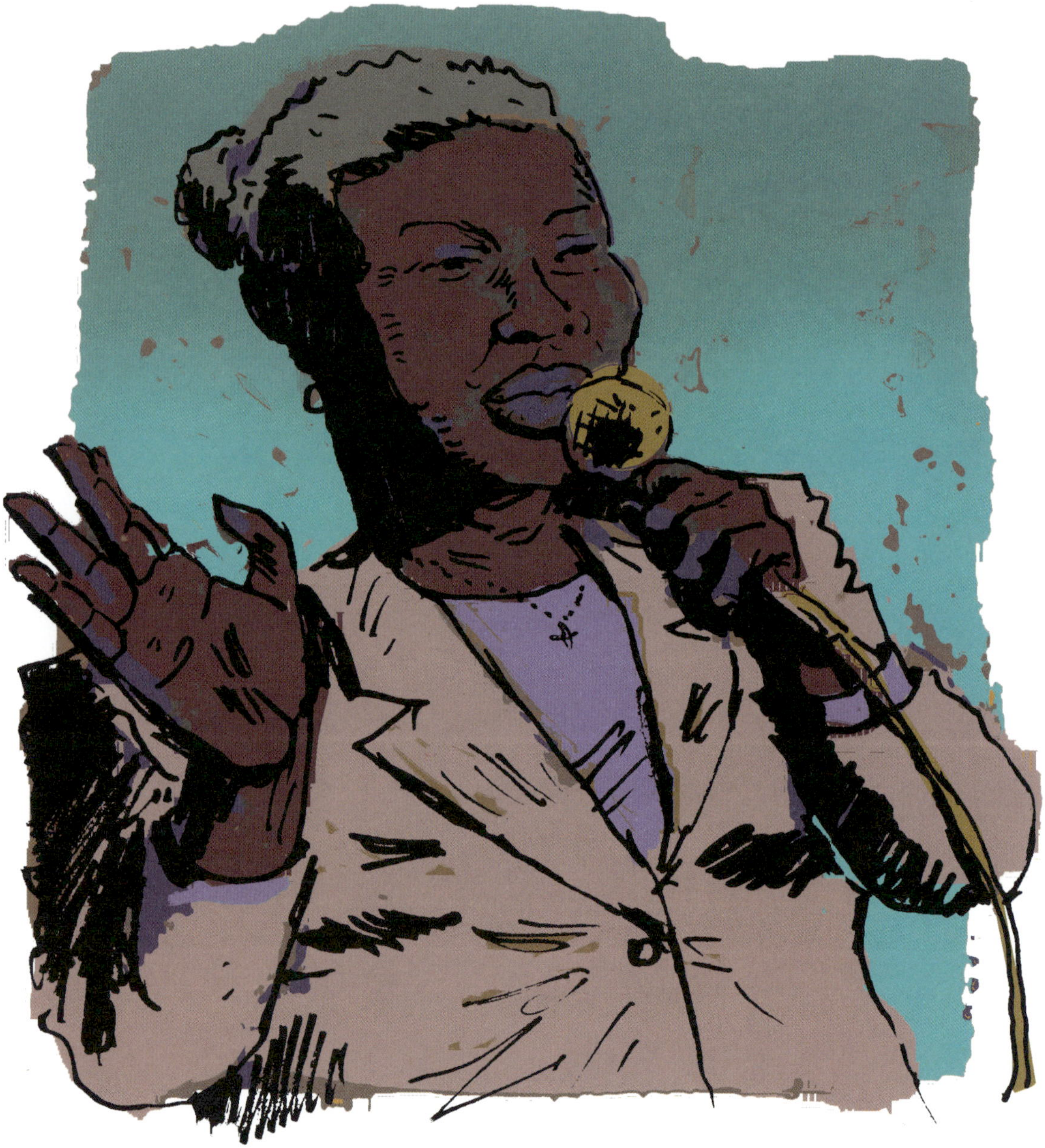

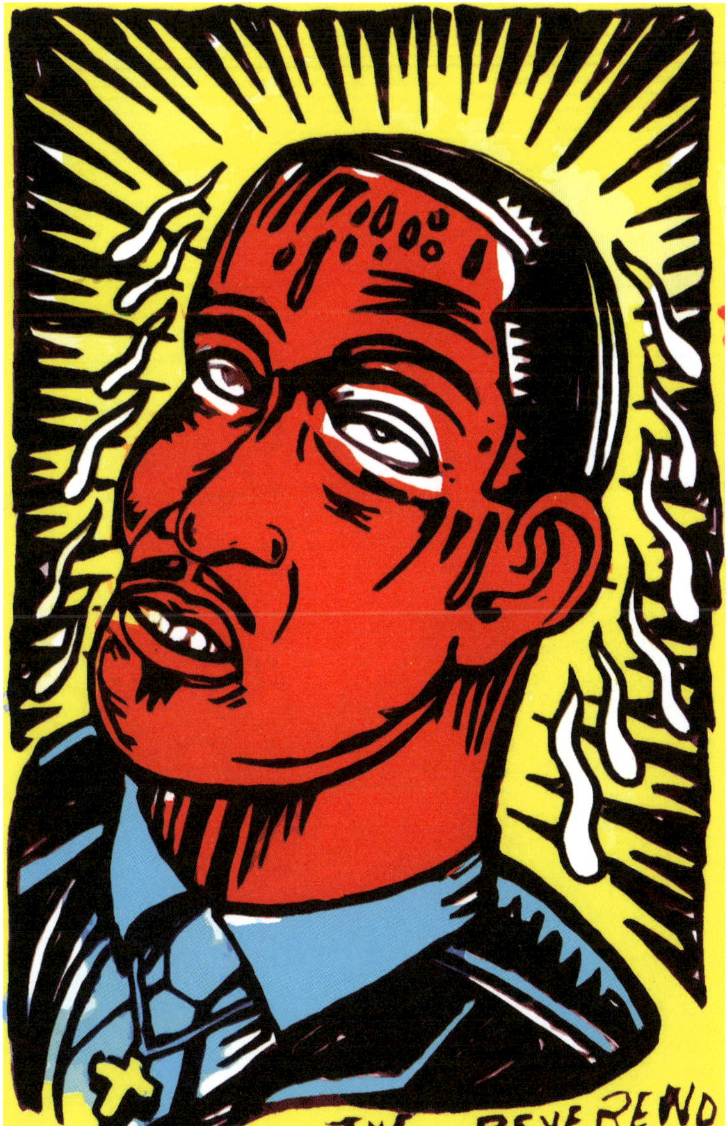
THE REVEREND

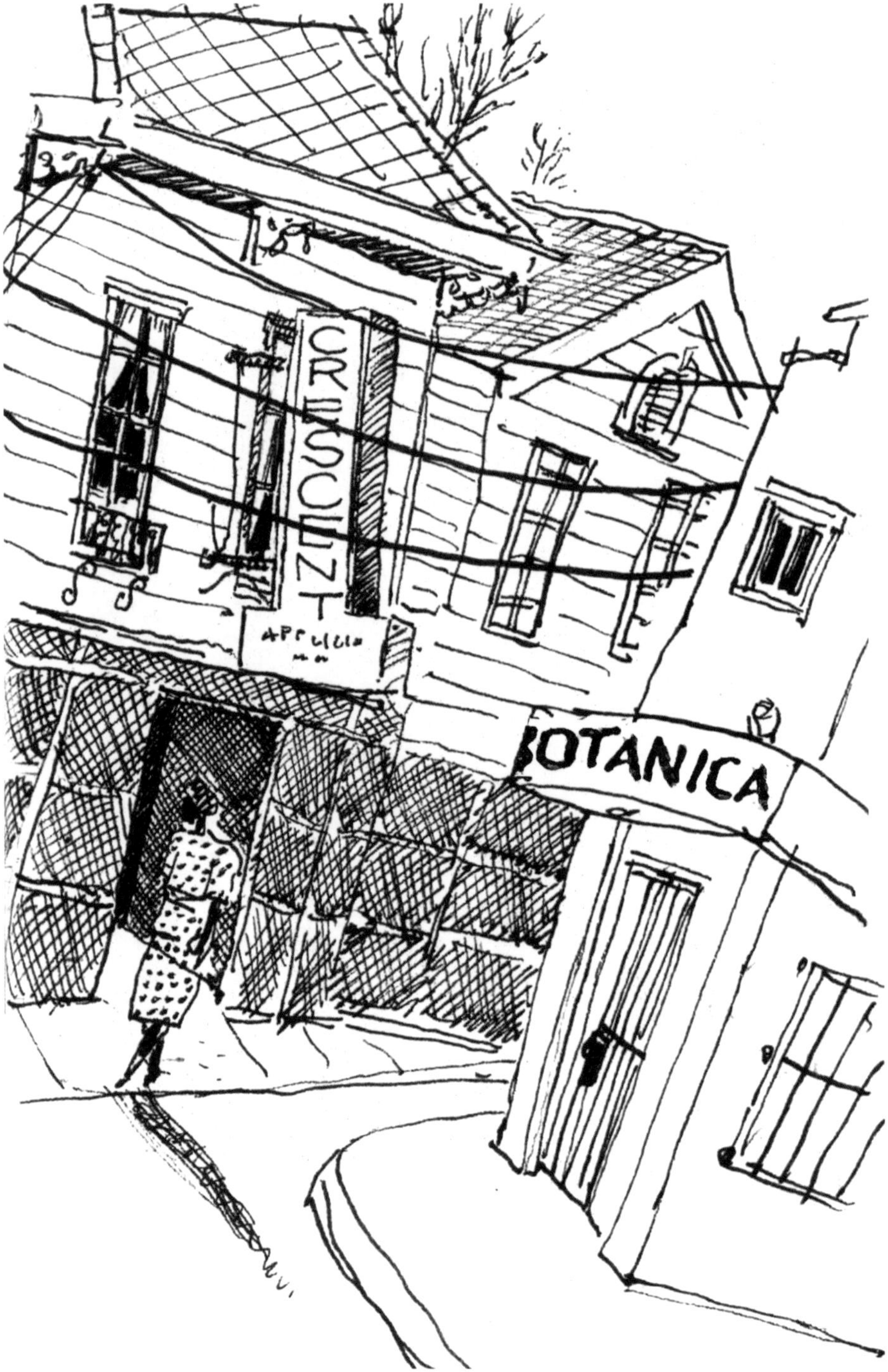
CRESCENT
OTANICA

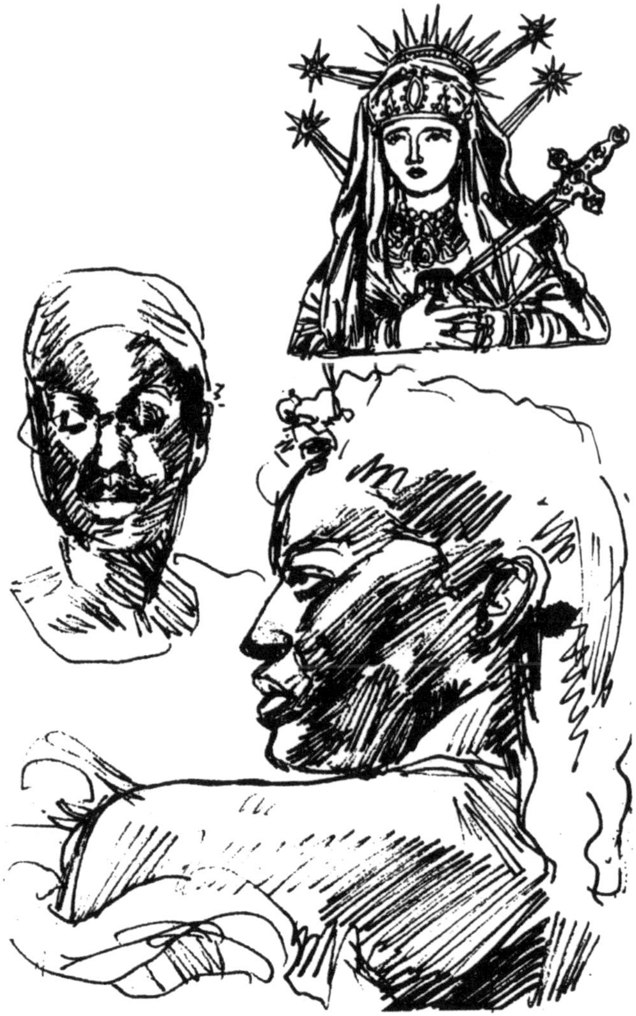



My VouDou Godmother, the Reverend Lorita Honeycutt Gamble, is a good friend of mine.
She ran a Botanica off Canal Street. You could buy a soda or you could buy a spell.
This wasn't tourist stuff but "The Religion" brought by African slaves merged with Caribbean Catholicism.
The survival of the soul. The belief in saints.
The power of possession by the Orisha—the VouDou gods.

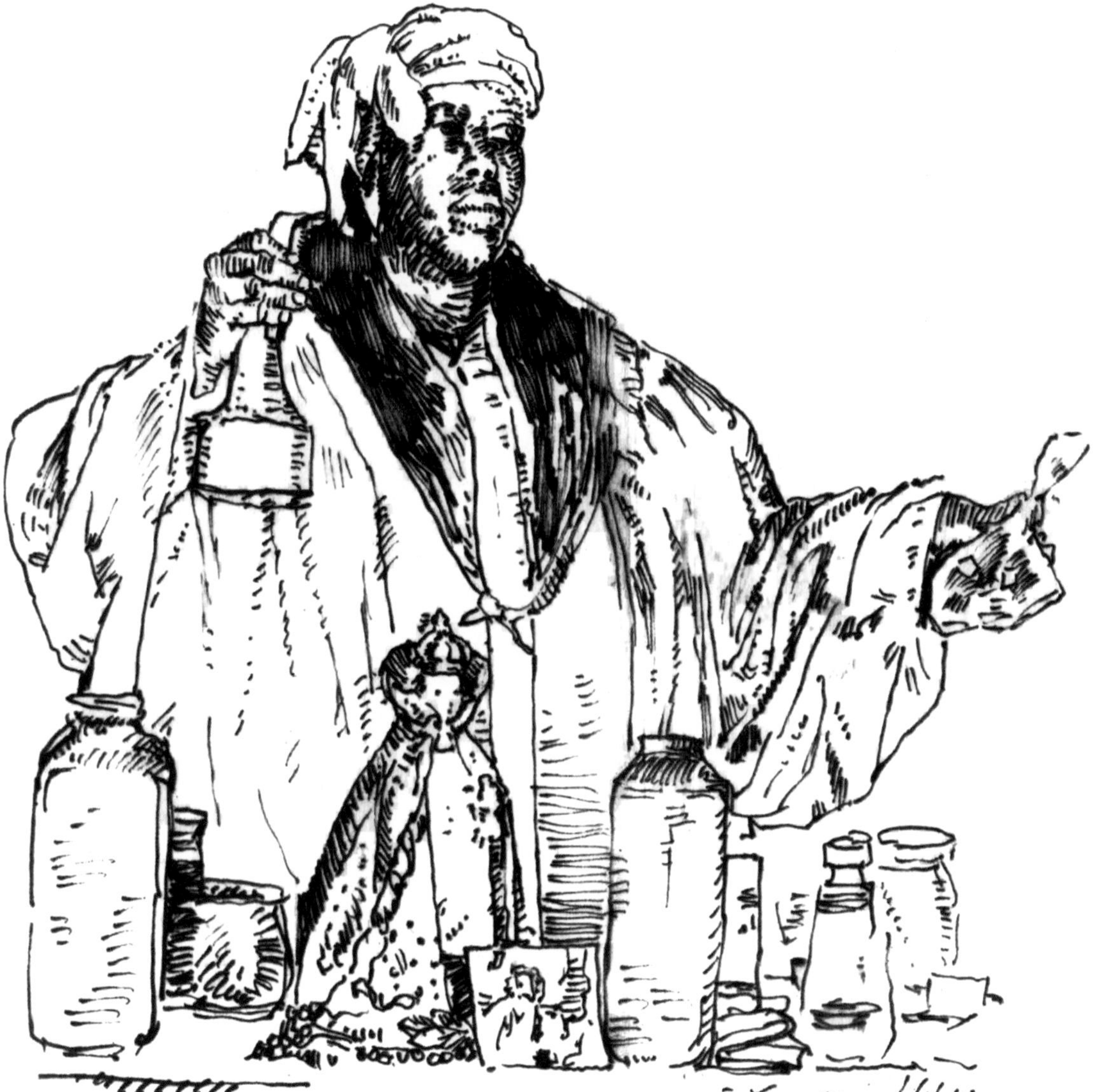

The VouDou ceremony.

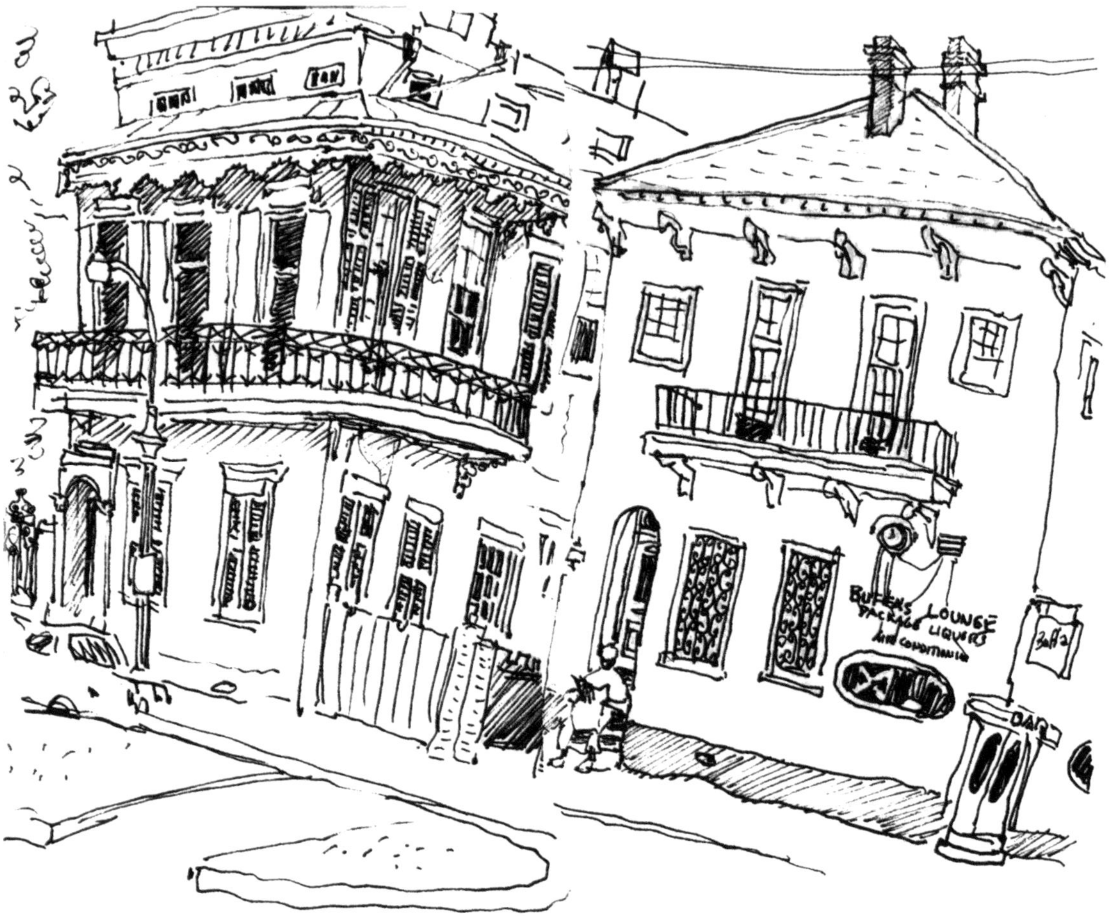



Esplanade Avenue.

THE POPULATION OF THIS CITY always knew they shared the land with ghosts of times past. You can count among those spirits the pirate Jean Lafitte, Buddy Bolden and Louis Armstrong; the fancy ladies of Storyville; the countless drifters and adventurers who came down the Mississippi River looking for work or trouble; and the elegant Creole families who carved civilization out of swampland; the French, Arcadians, Spanish, English, Germans, and later the Irish and Sicilians. And, of course, the slaves and Free People of Color who brought their own Afro-Caribbean secrets to this wild place.

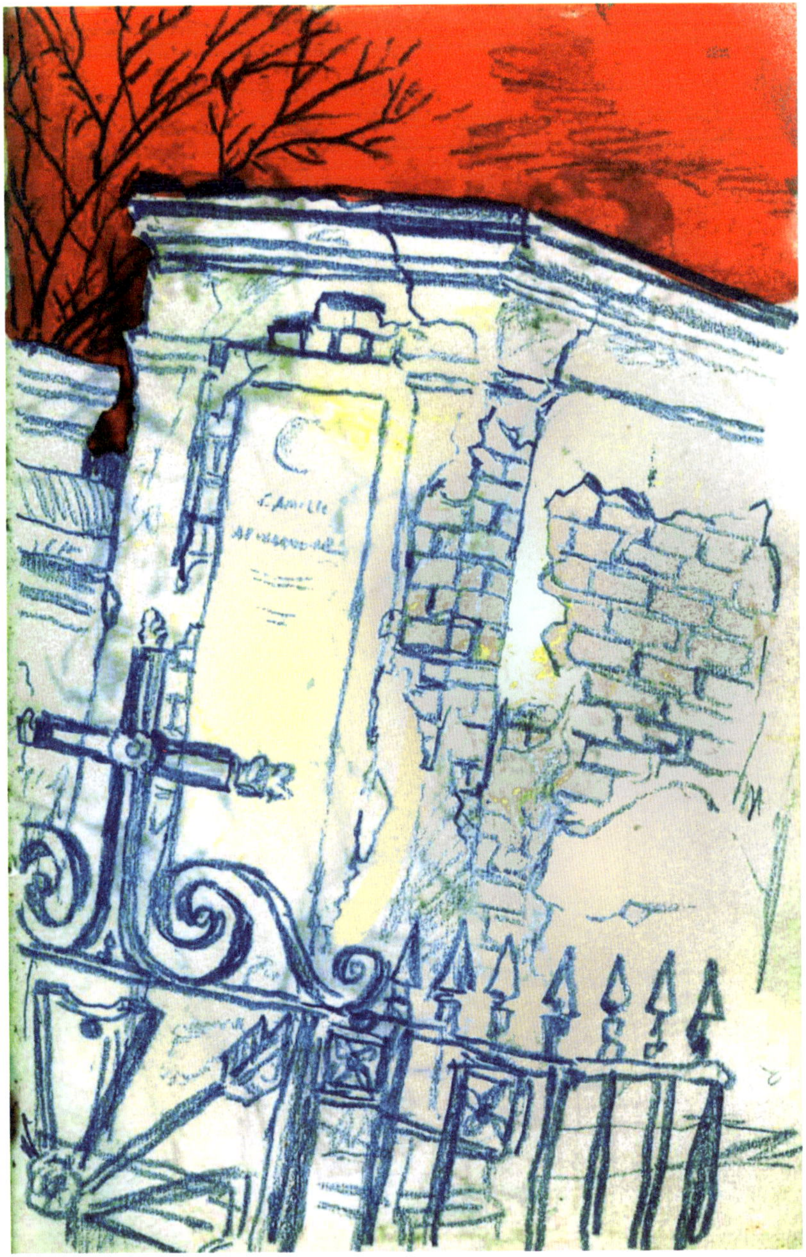

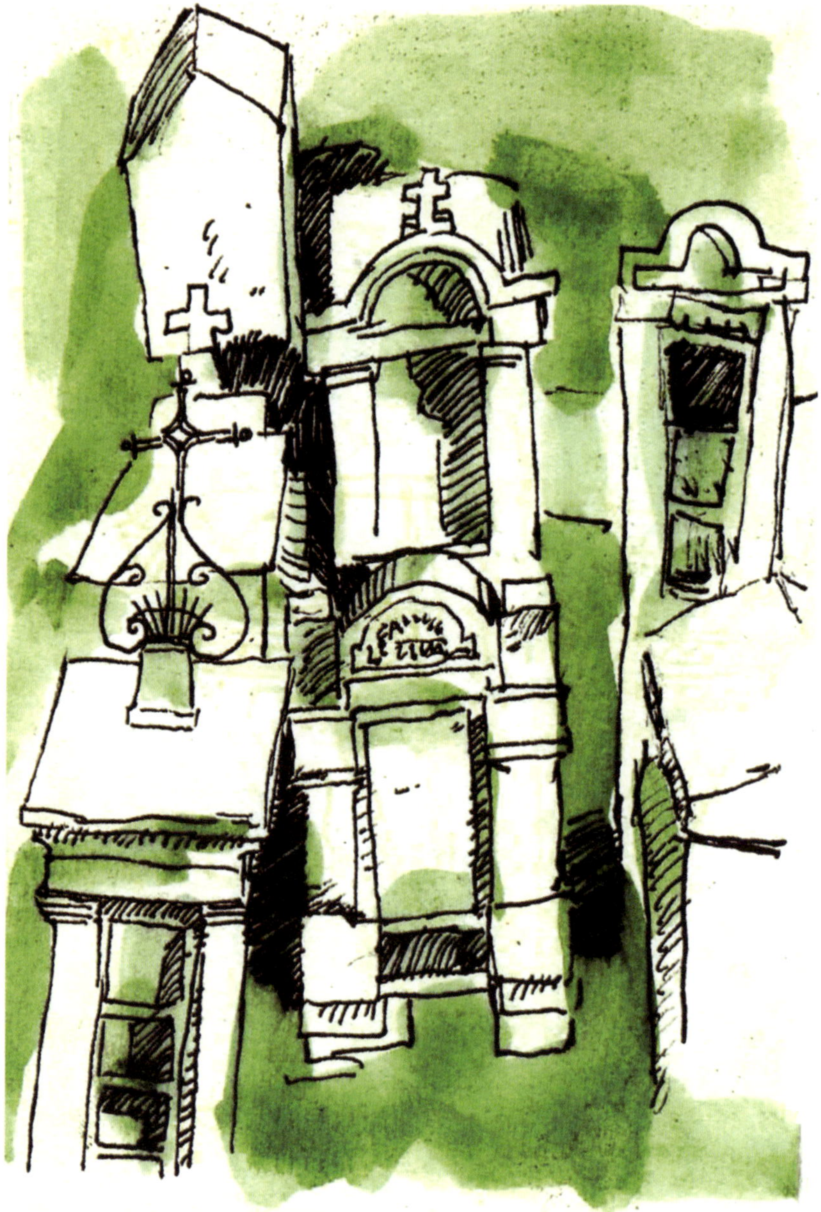

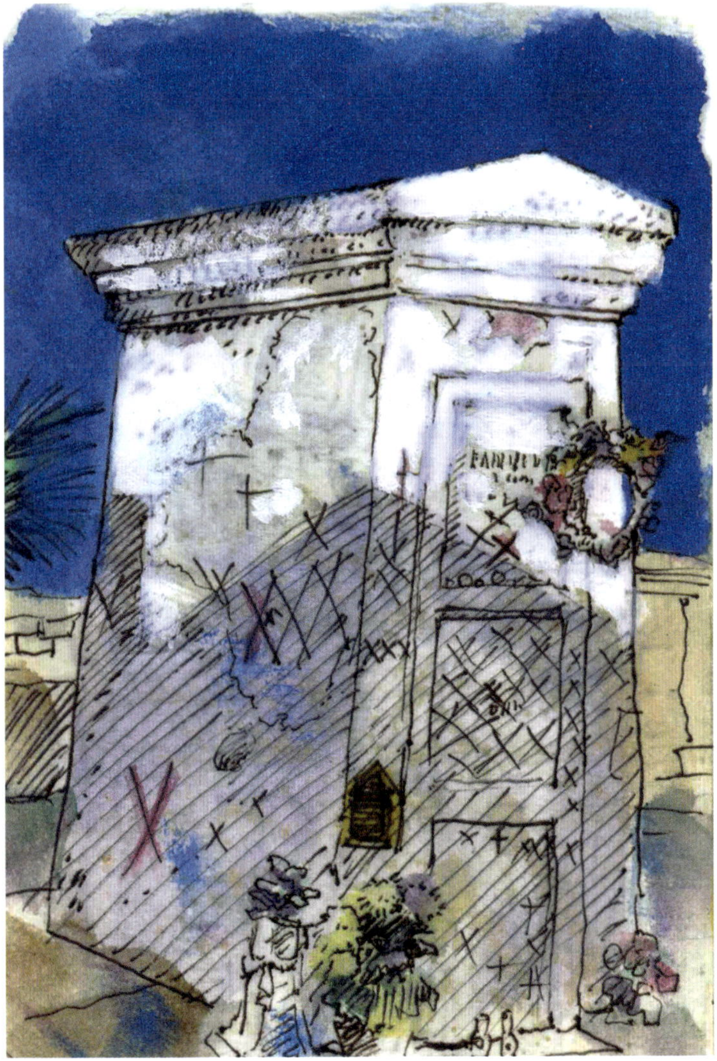

Tomb of "The Widow Paris" Marie Laveau,
the legendary Voodoo Queen in St. Louis Cemetery Number One off North Rampart Street.

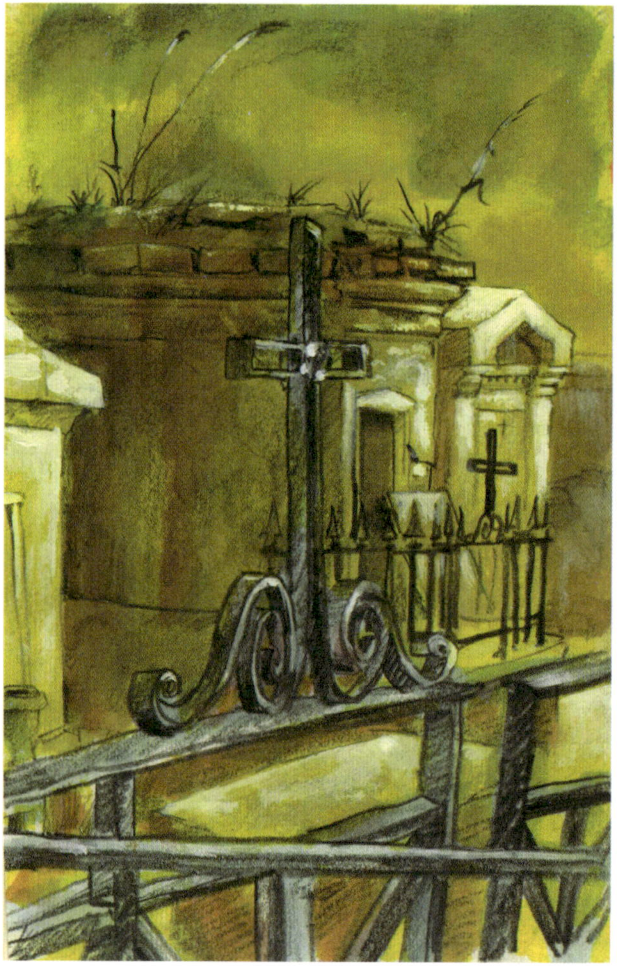



The Saint Louis cemeteries on the outskirts of the Quarter.

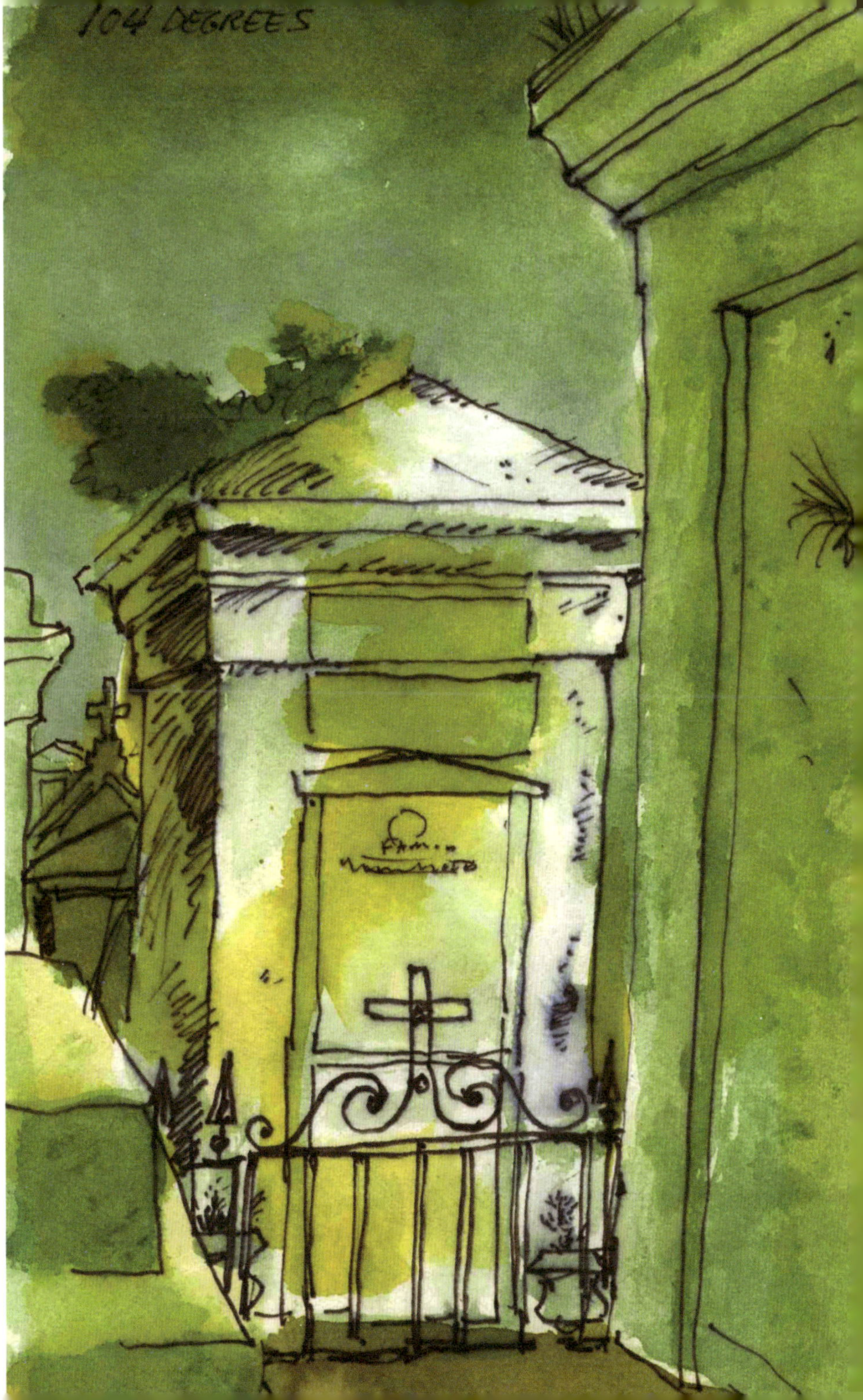
104 DEGREES

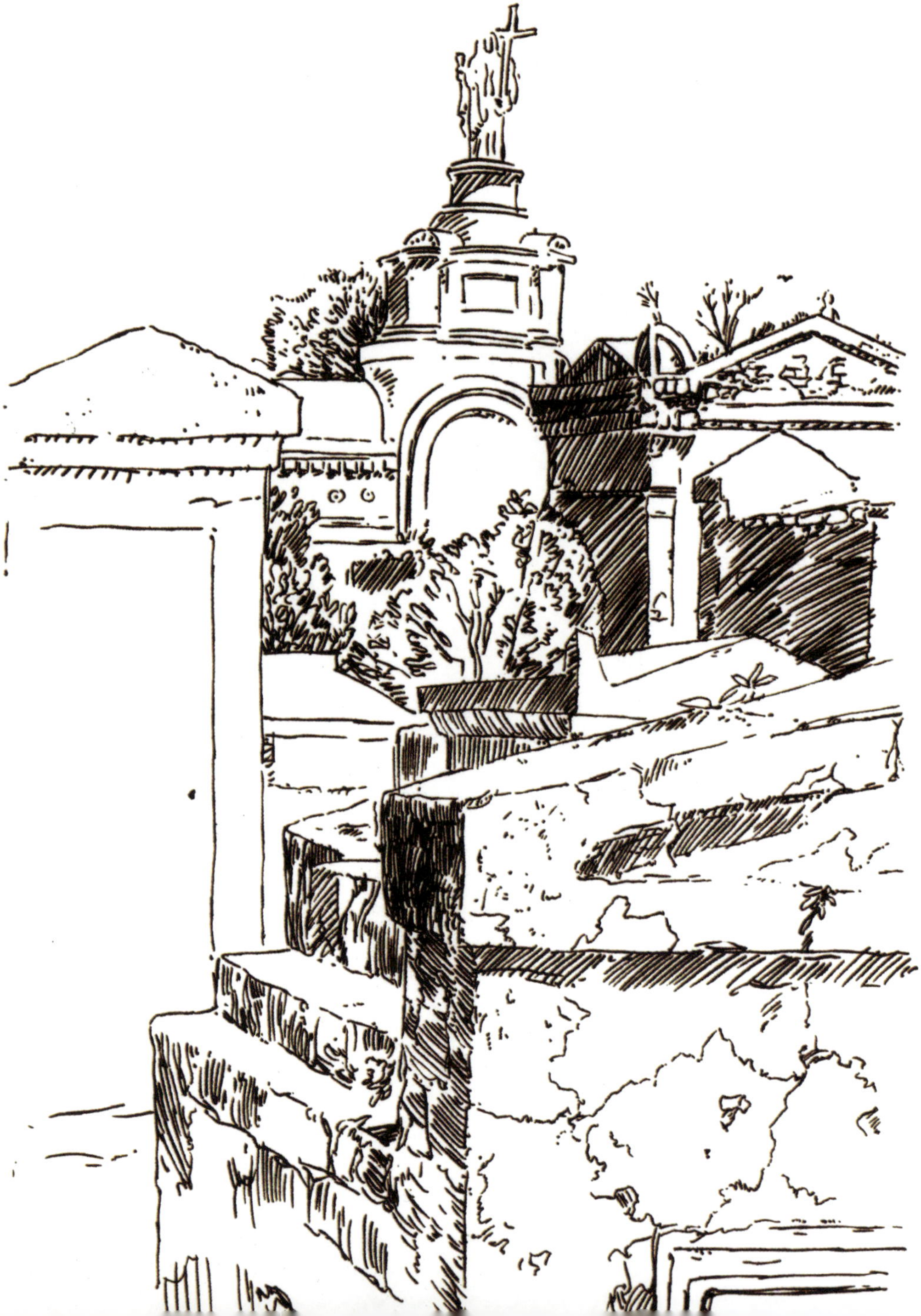

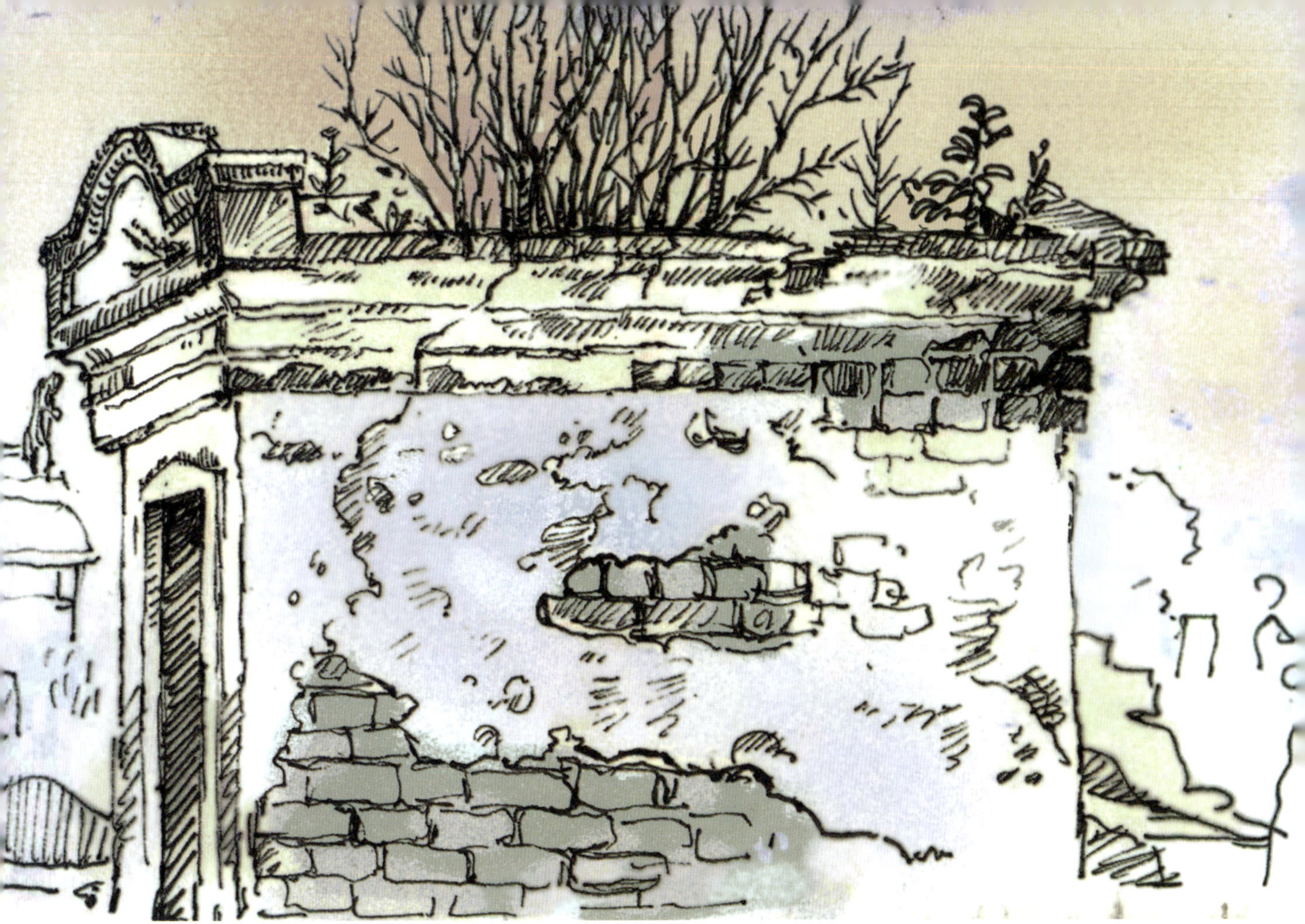



Where VouDou ladies get their graveyard dust for spells.

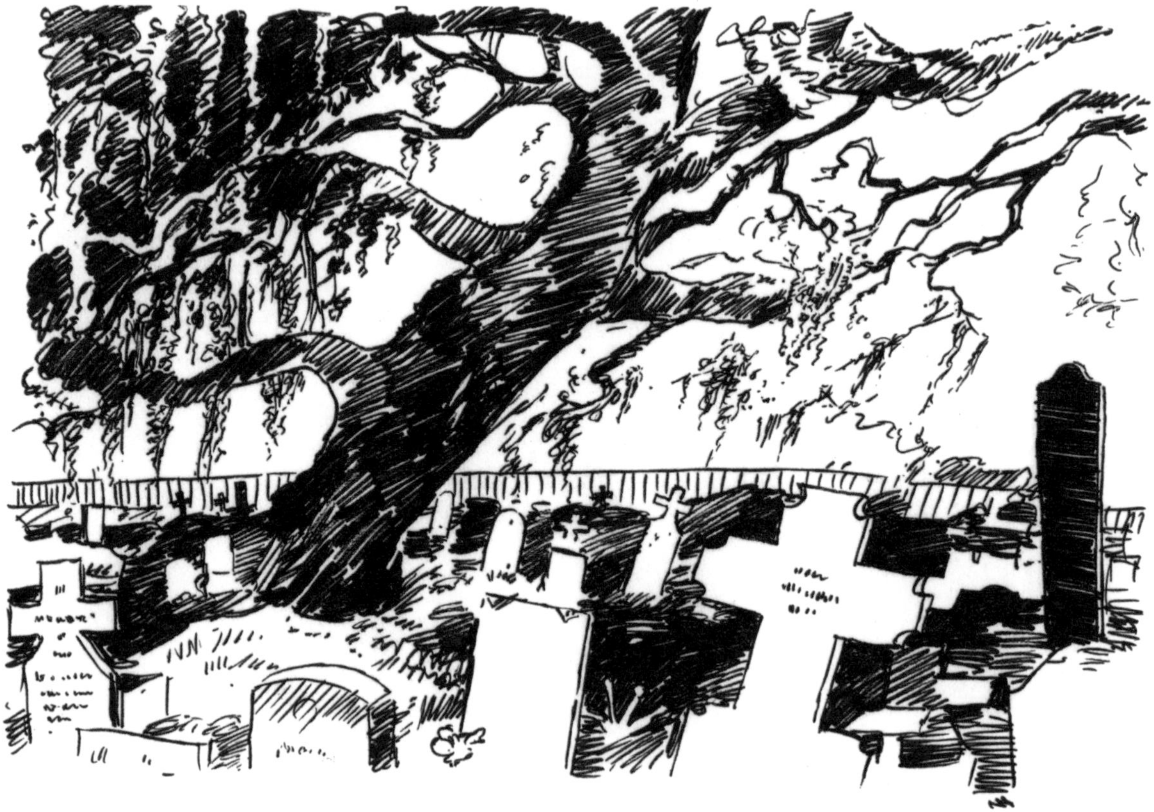



Holt Cemetery is the poor people's cemetery—the resting place of Buddy Bolden, the inventor of jazz music.
If you listen carefully you can almost hear the trumpet sound in the rustle of
the Spanish moss hanging from that big tree.

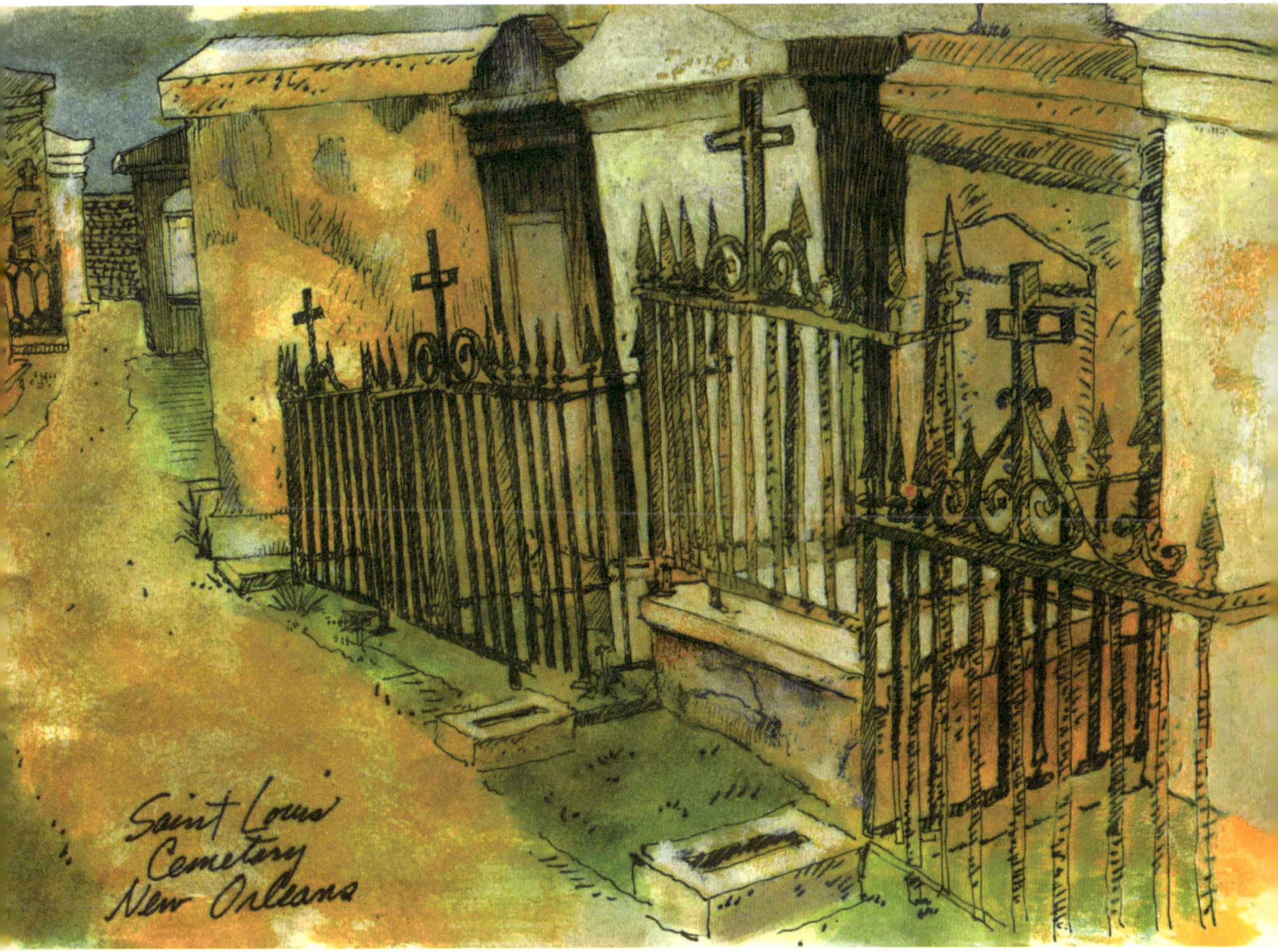
Saint Louis
Cemetery
New Orleans

A LOT HAS BEEN WRITTEN ABOUT JAZZ, the single most celebrated characteristic of New Orleans. So I needn't write much more about it.

It would take page after page just to name the famous New Orleans musicians and their wonderful contributions to the world at large.

And what would the world be like without jazz, without New Orleans?

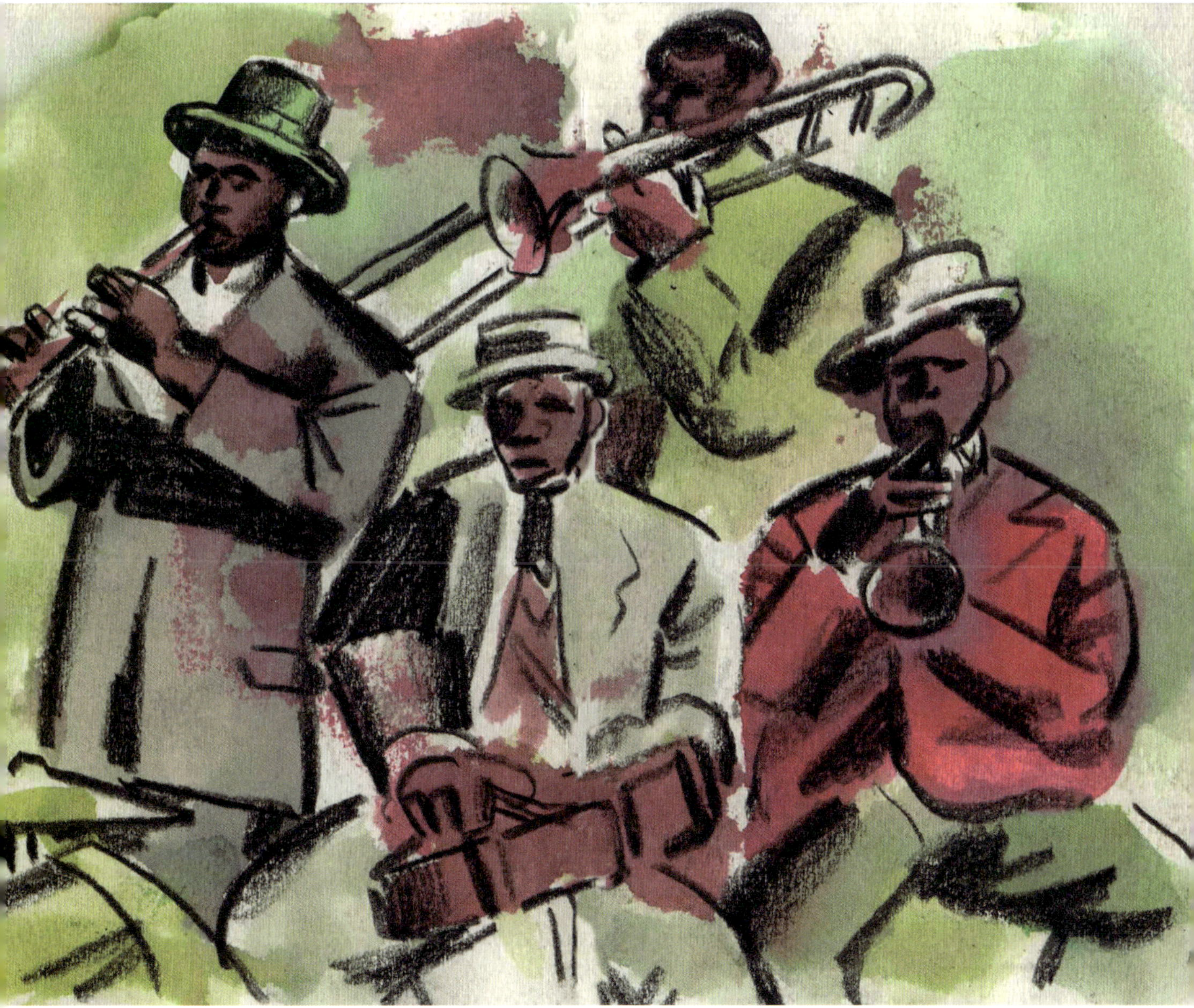

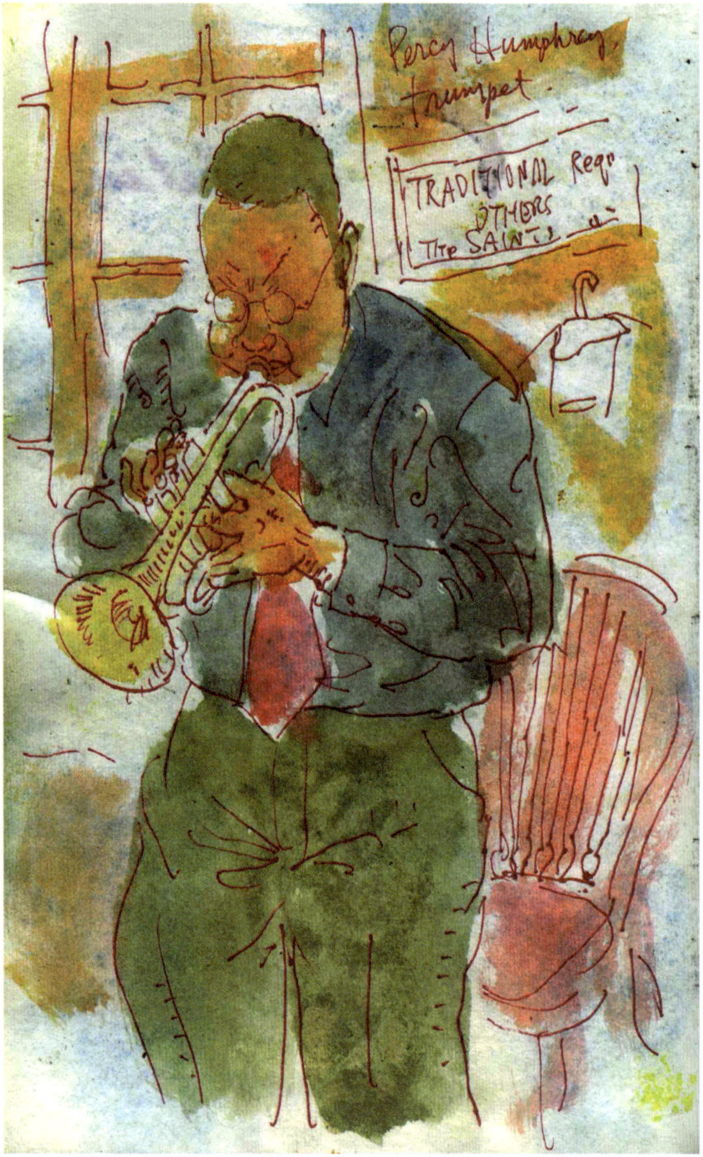
Percy Humphrey,
trumpet
TRADITIONAL Req
OTHERS
The SAINTS

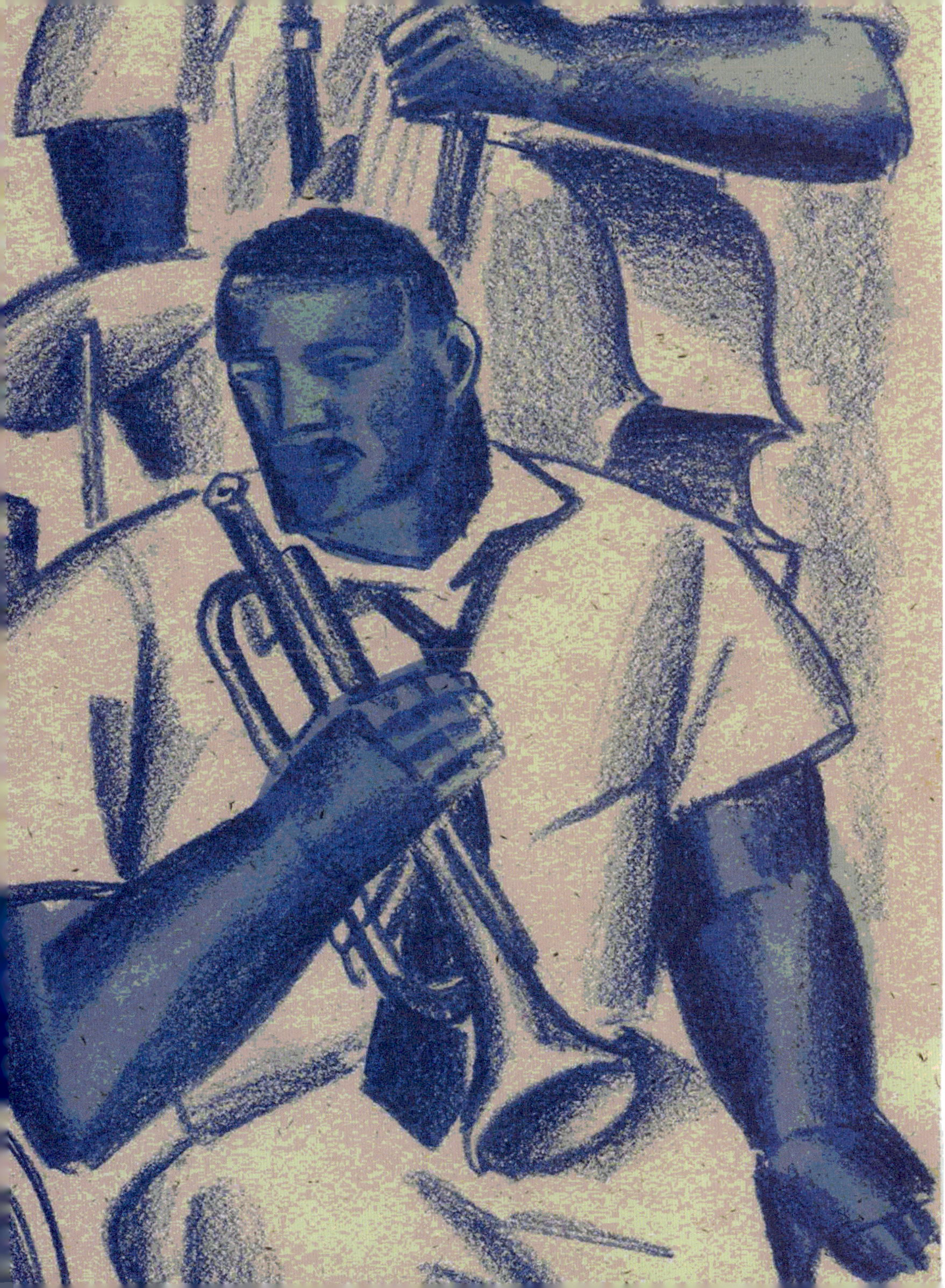

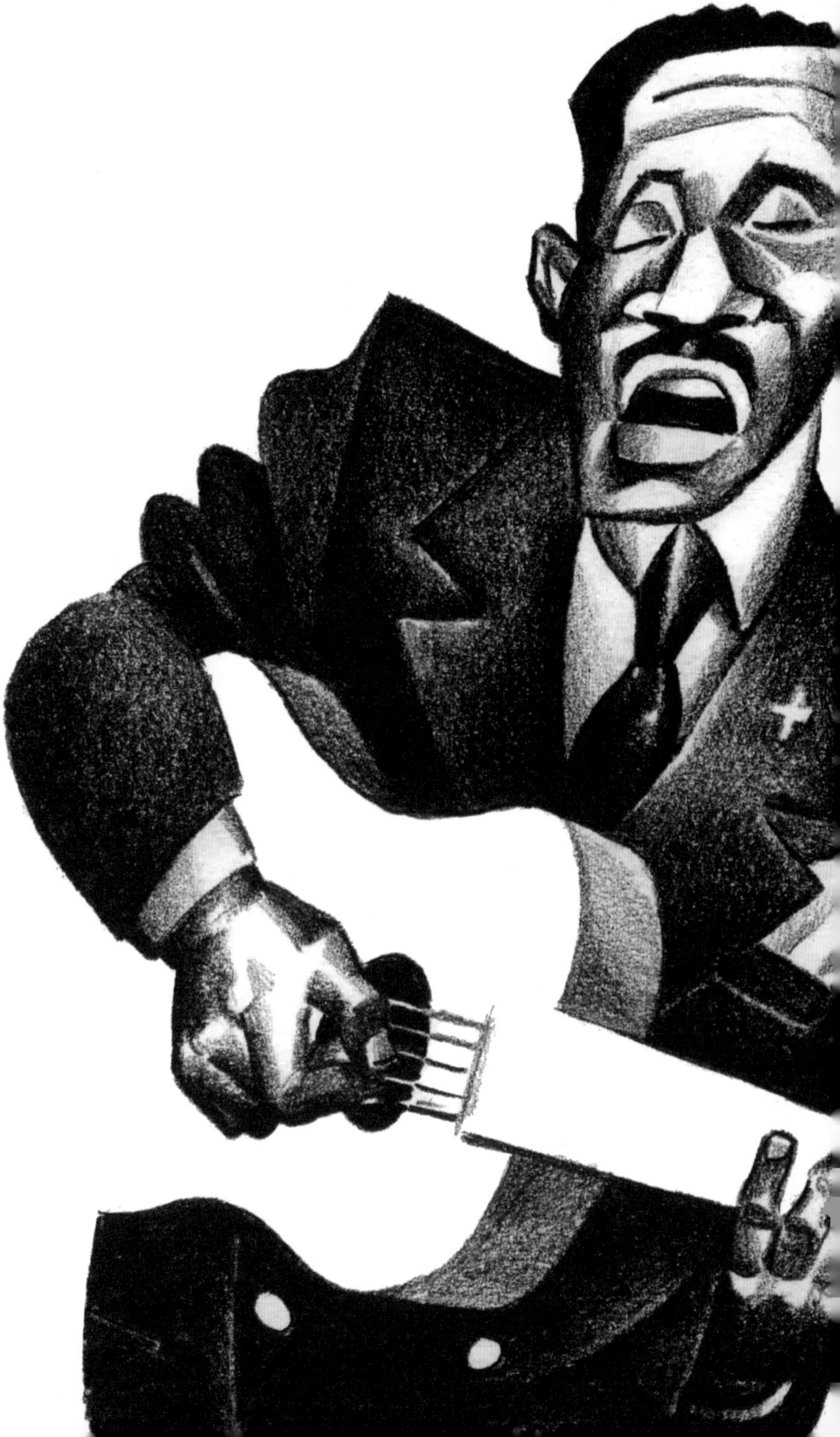

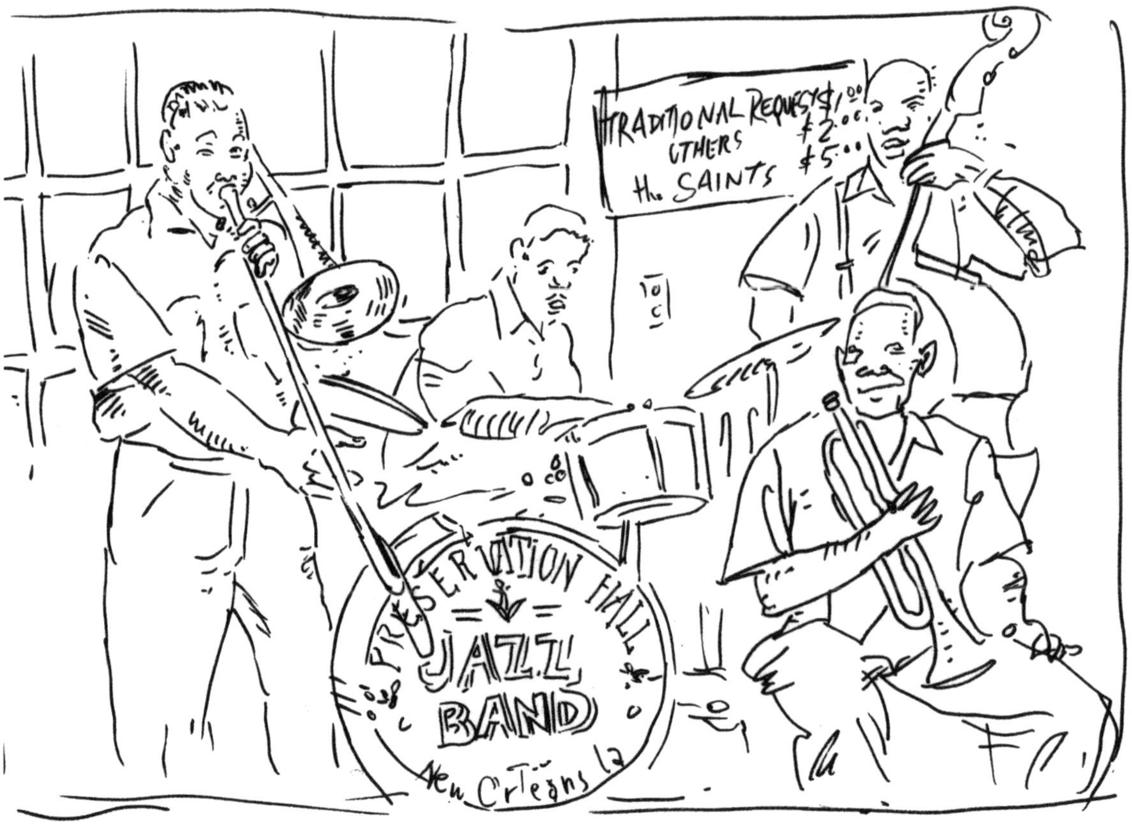




Dixieland Jazz at Preservation Hall.

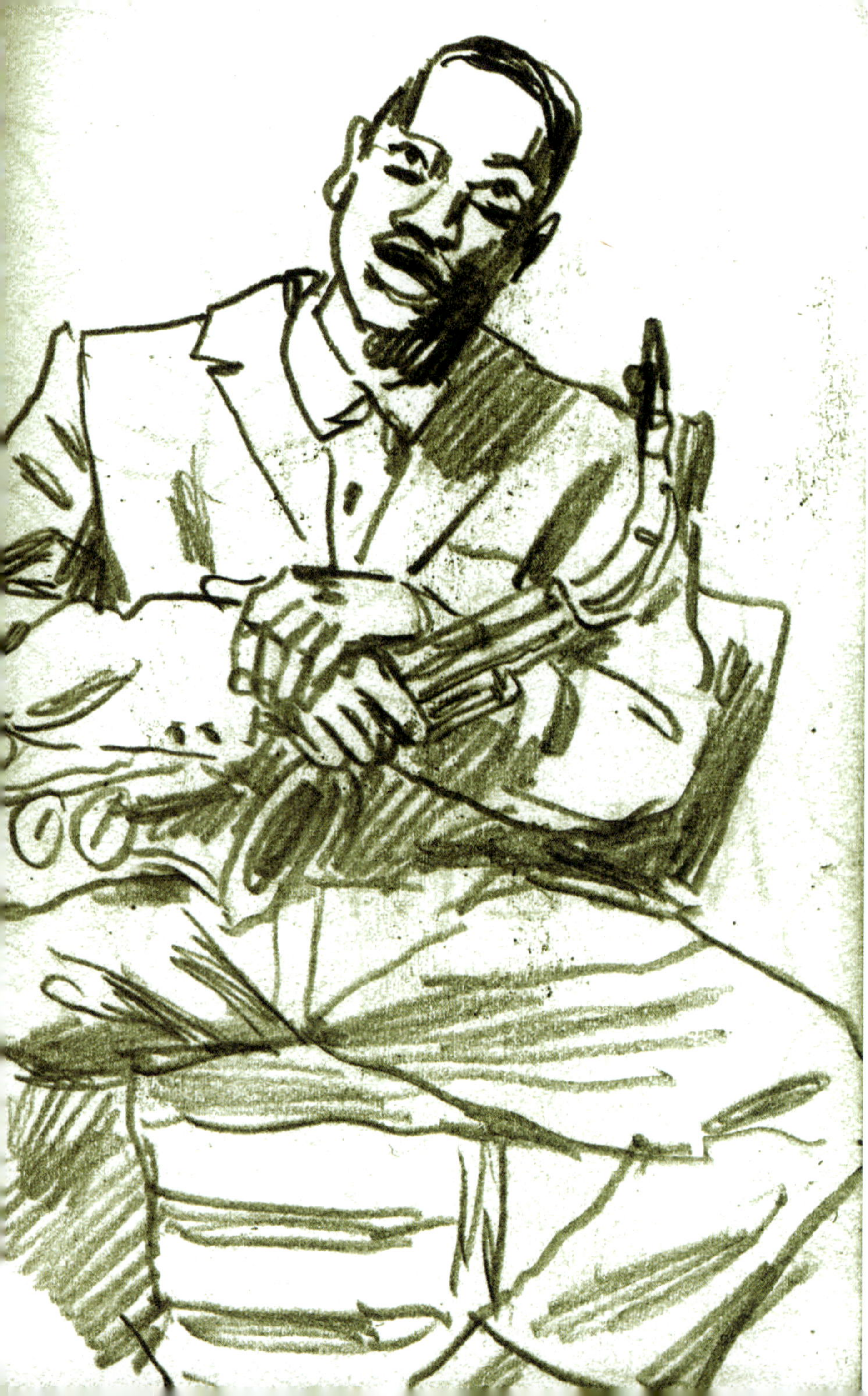

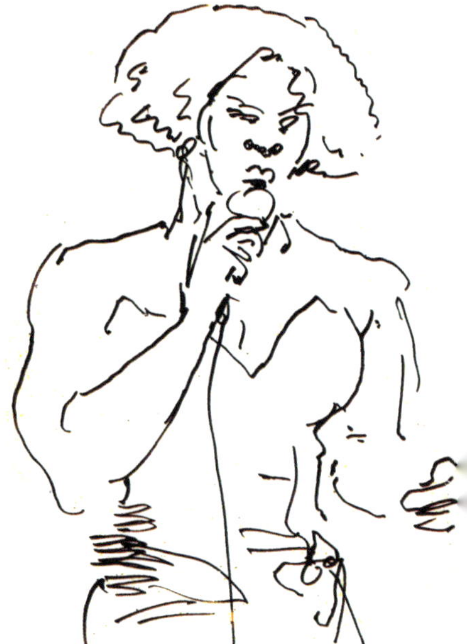

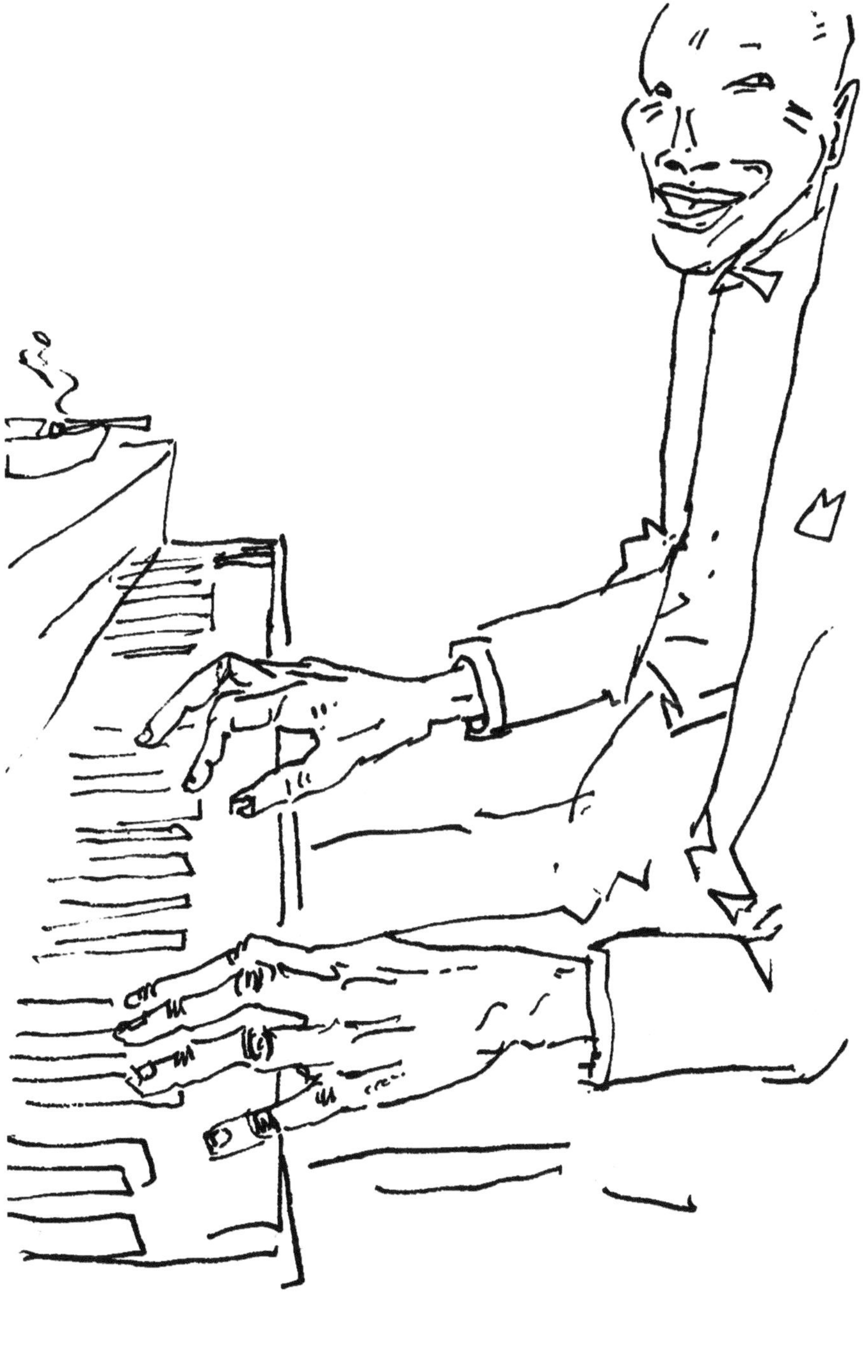

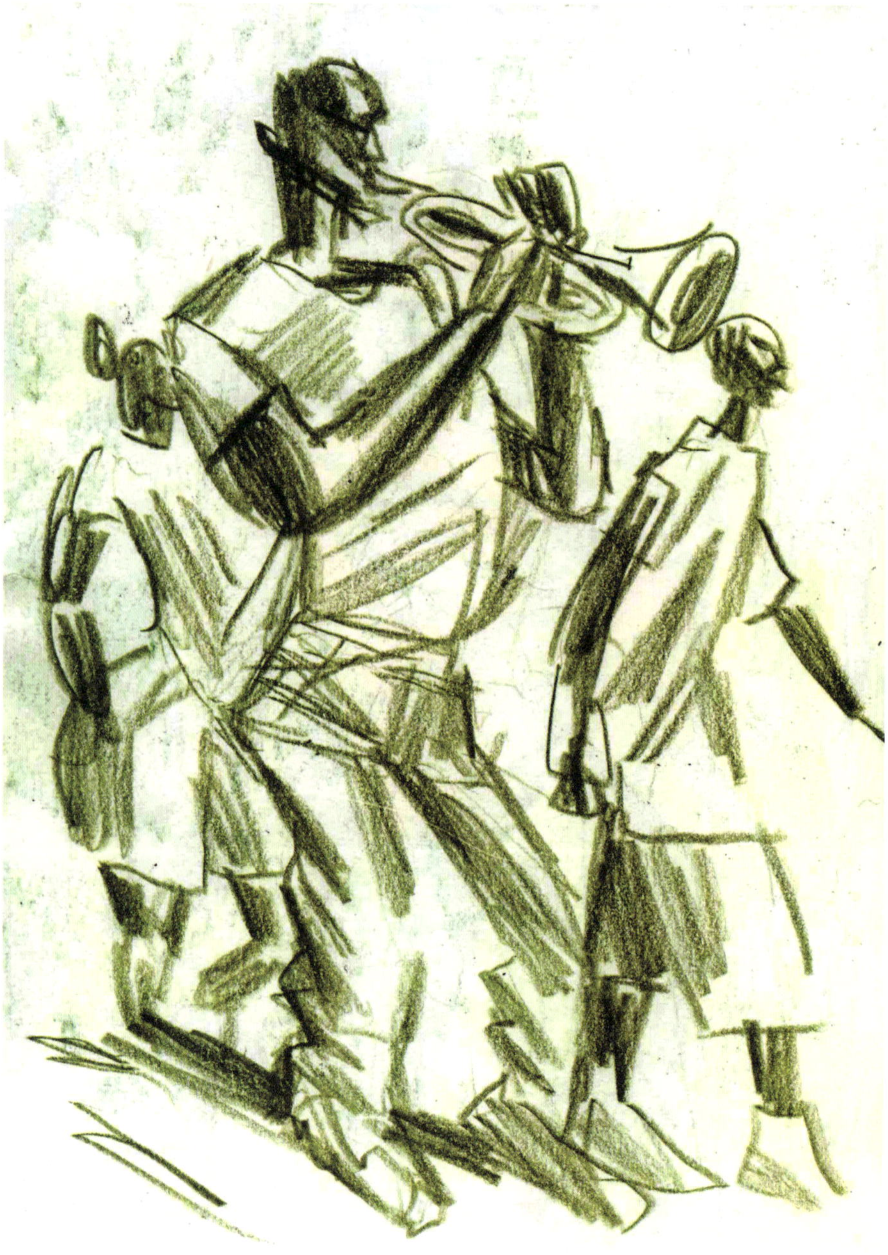

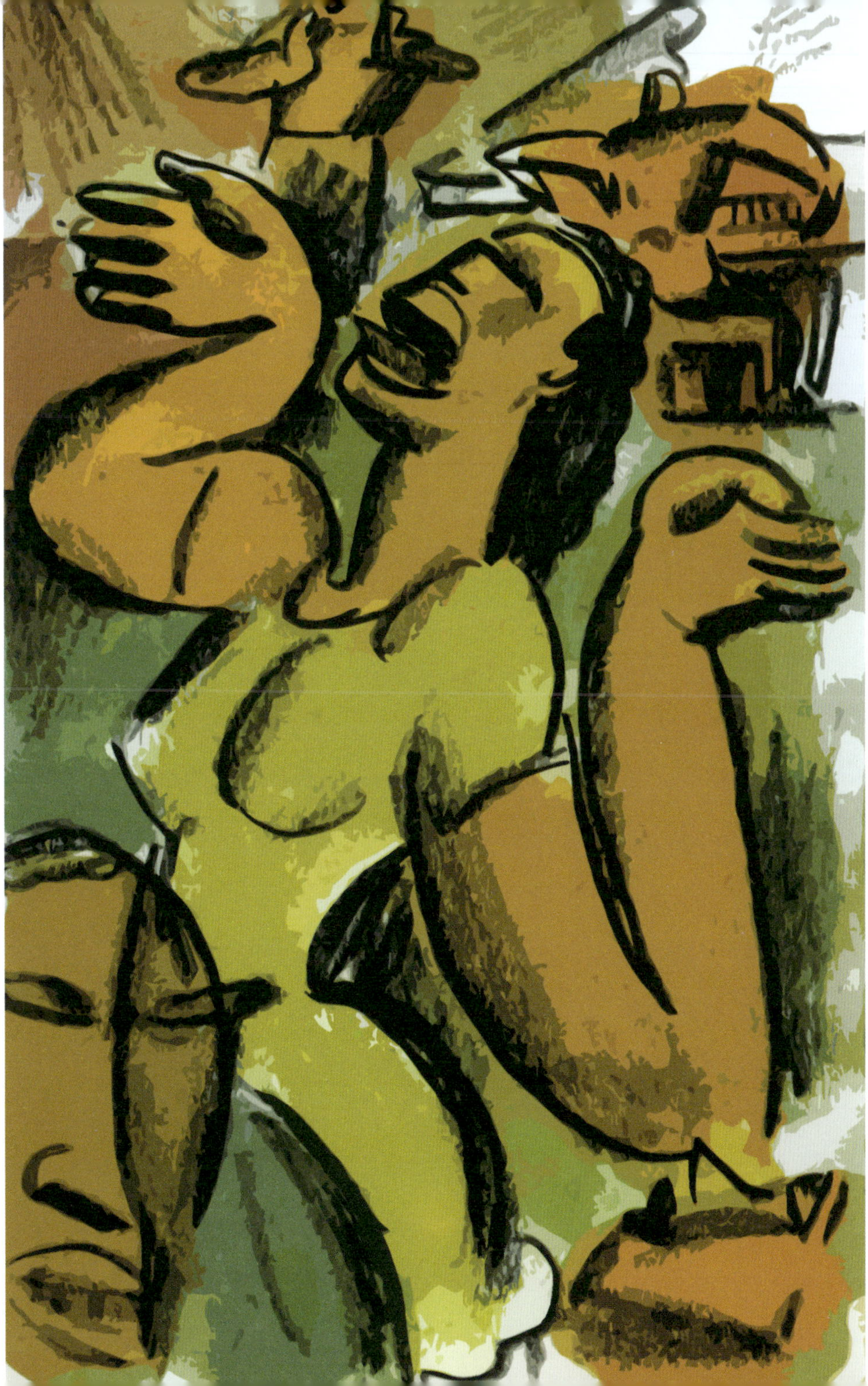

MERMAIDS, TIN MEN, HELL HOUNDS, plumed birds, Martians, courtiers, Vikings, pirates, cavewomen, vampires, devils, angels, bunnies, skeletons, ballerinas, catwomen, werewolves, centaurs, Carmen Mirandas, pharaohs, musketeers, crawfish, Teletubbies, robots, courtesans, leather boys, Amazon queens, Greek gods, geisha girls, harlequins, Biblical prophets, drunken university students dressed up like beer cans, and beautiful creatures with gossamer wings.

Mardi Gras is America's version of Rome's Saturnalia. A kind of walking, talking Surrealism.

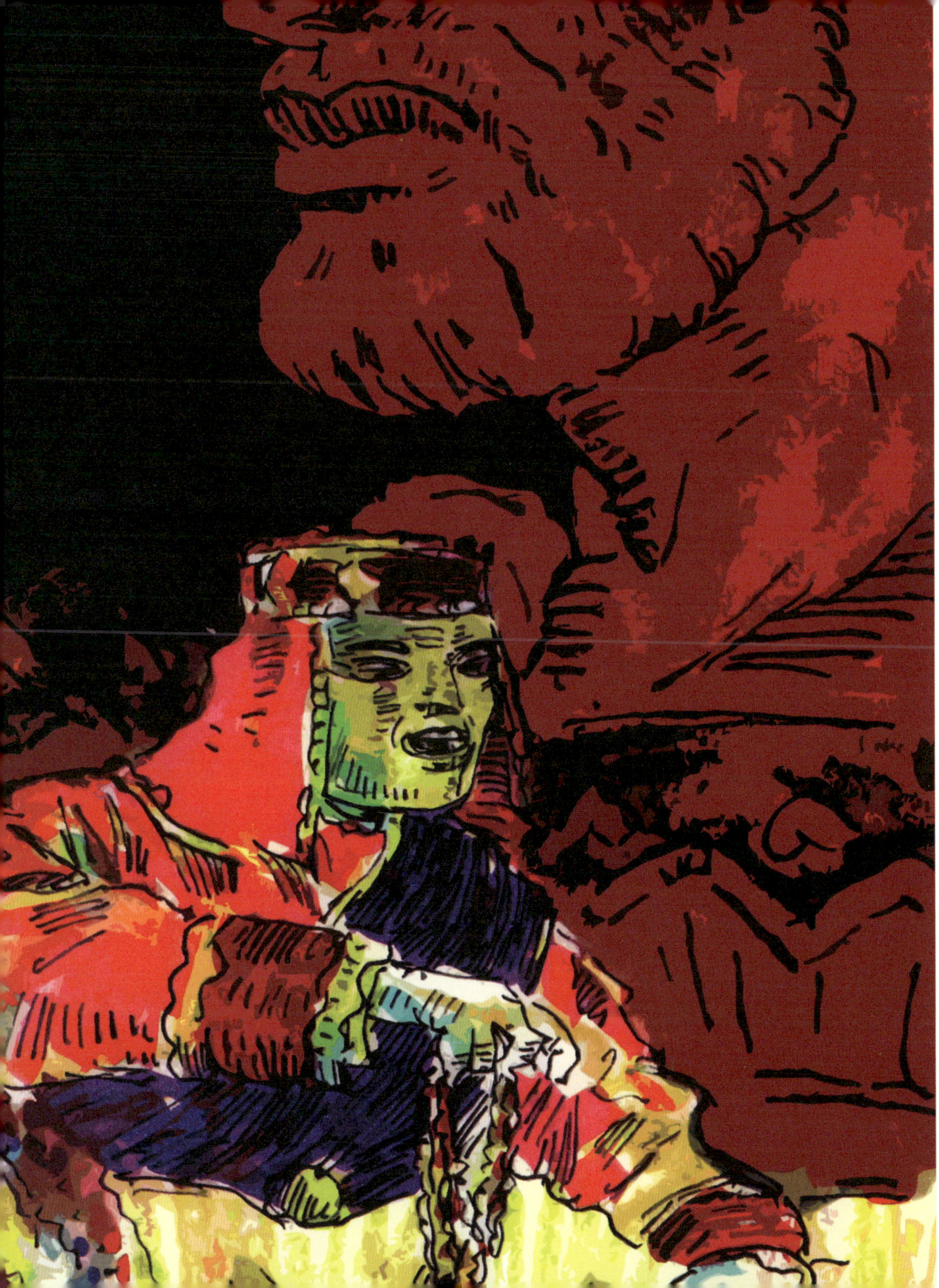

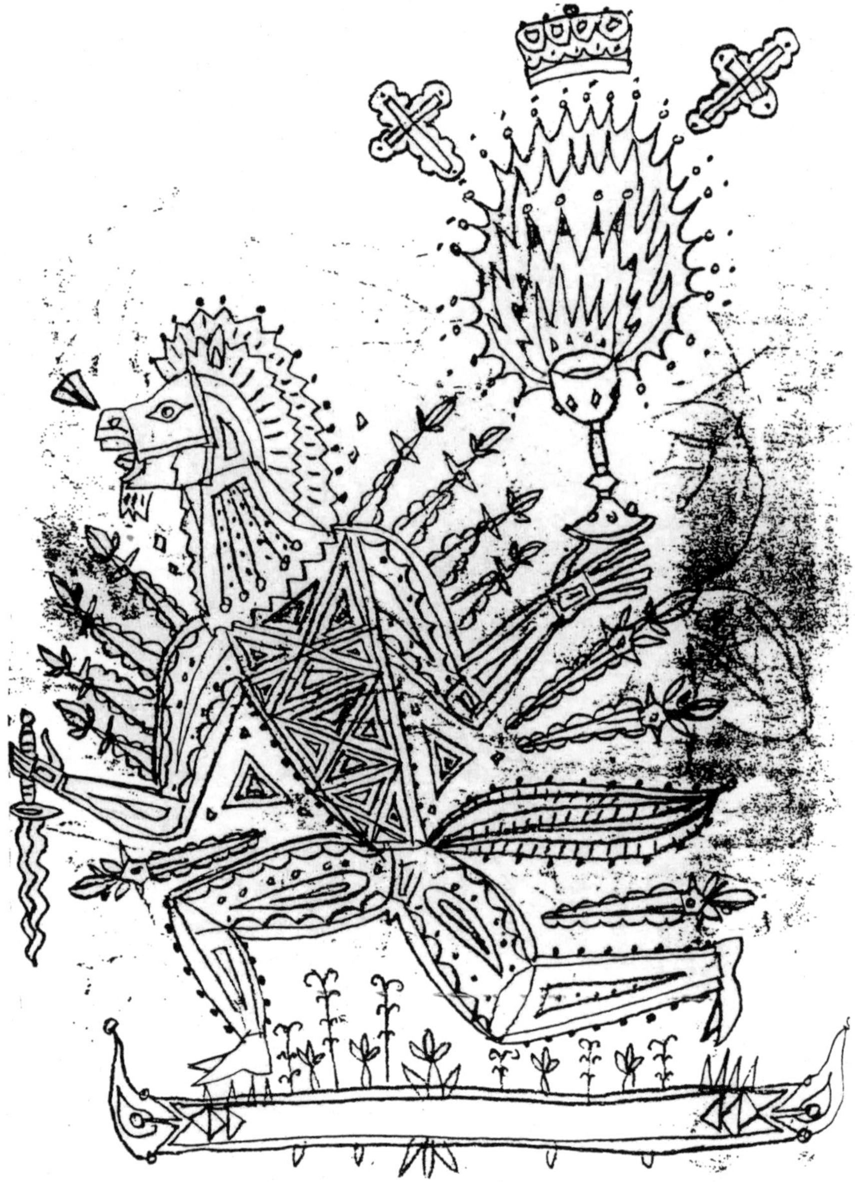

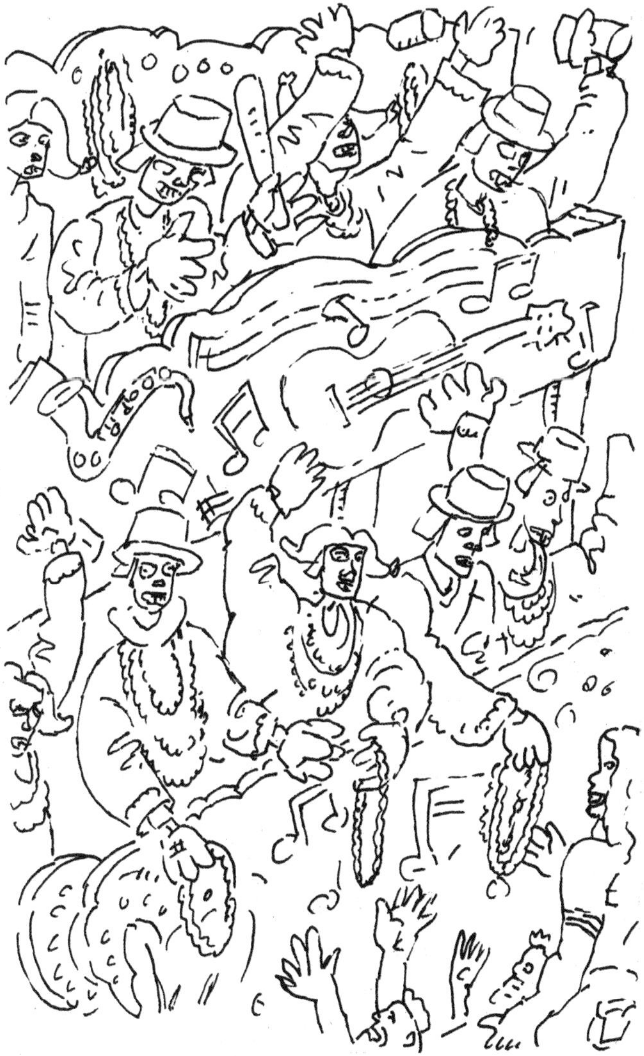



Like all the Carnival festivities worldwide,
from Venice to Rio,
"Fat Tuesday" is essentially a religious festival before Lent.

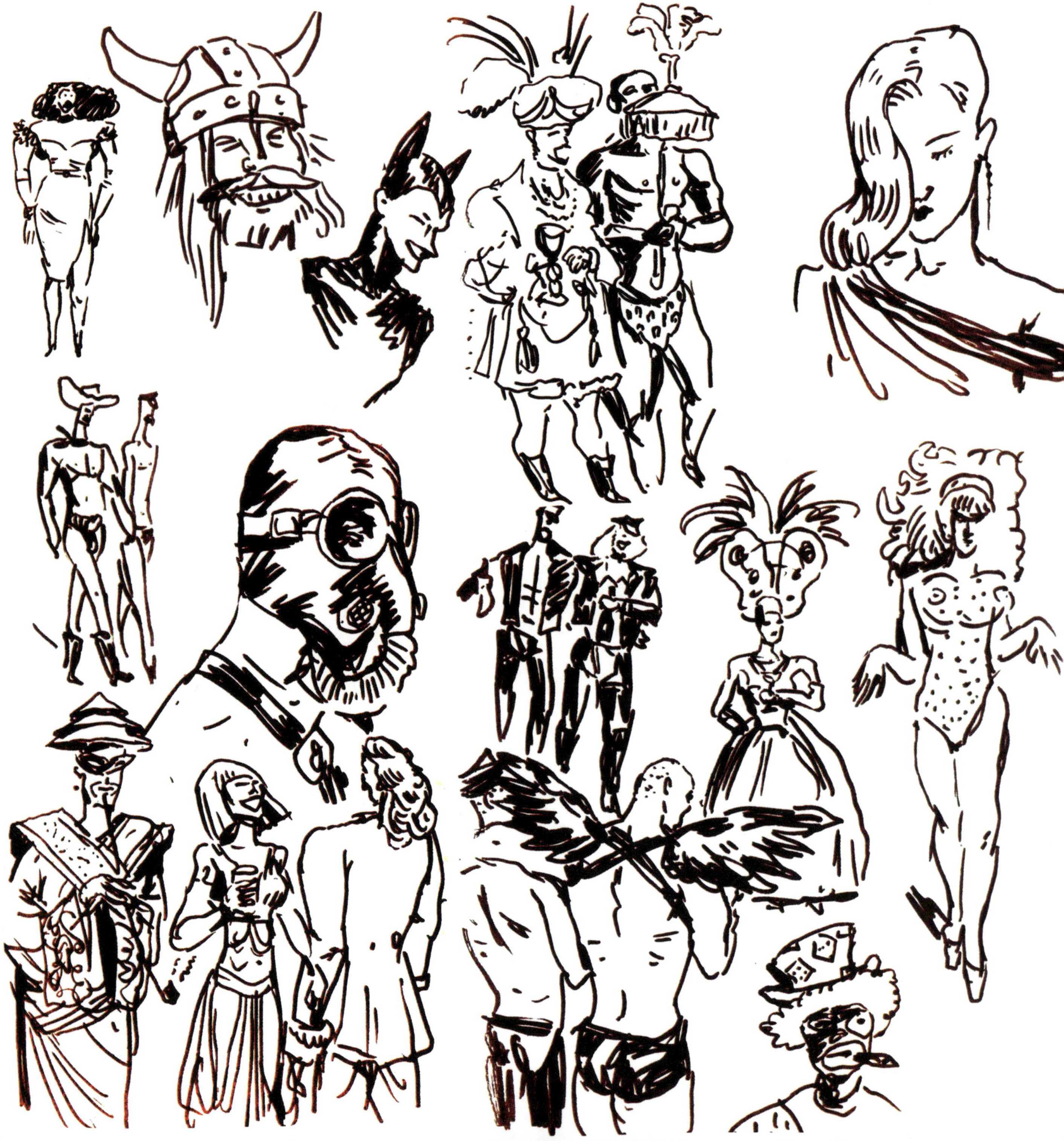

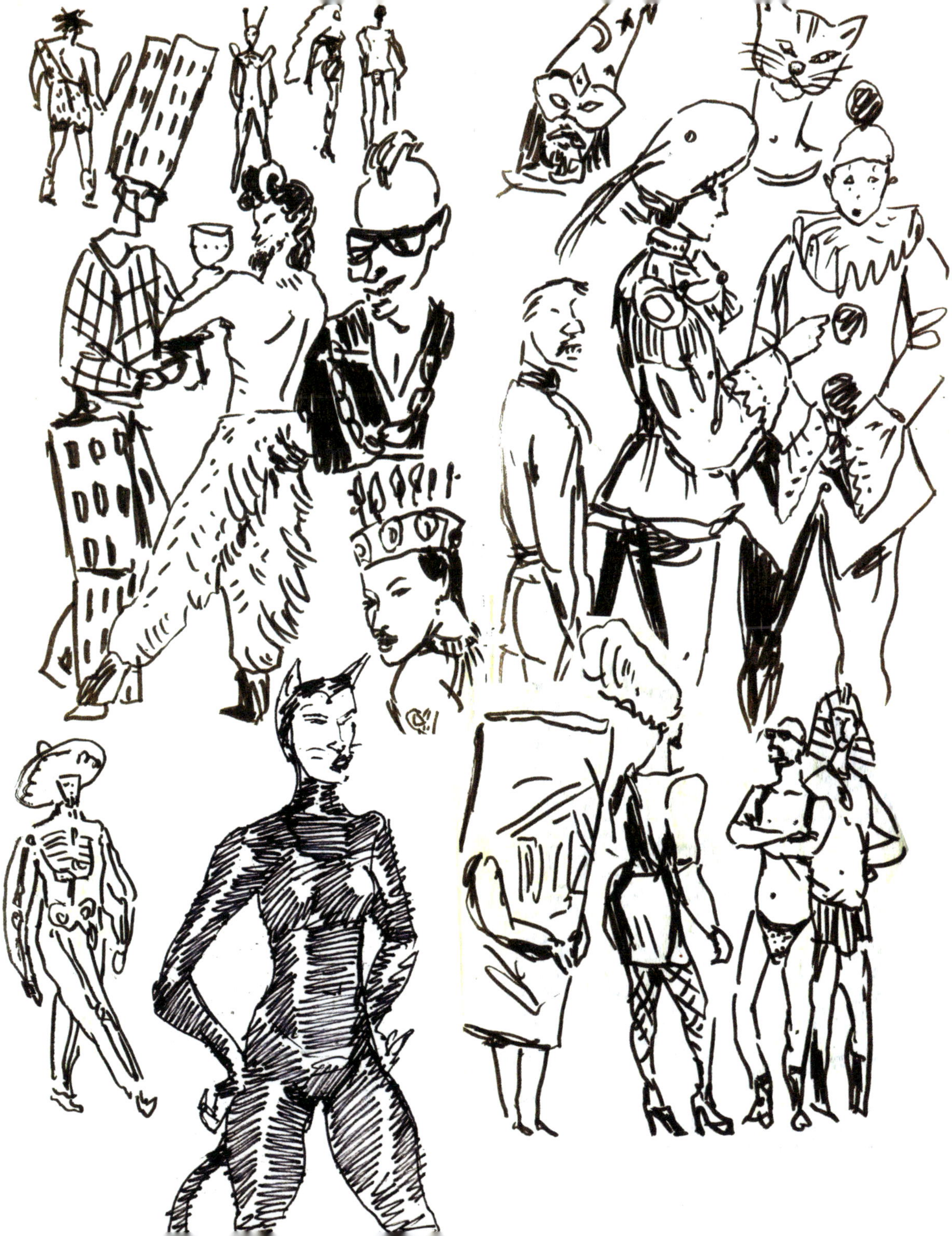

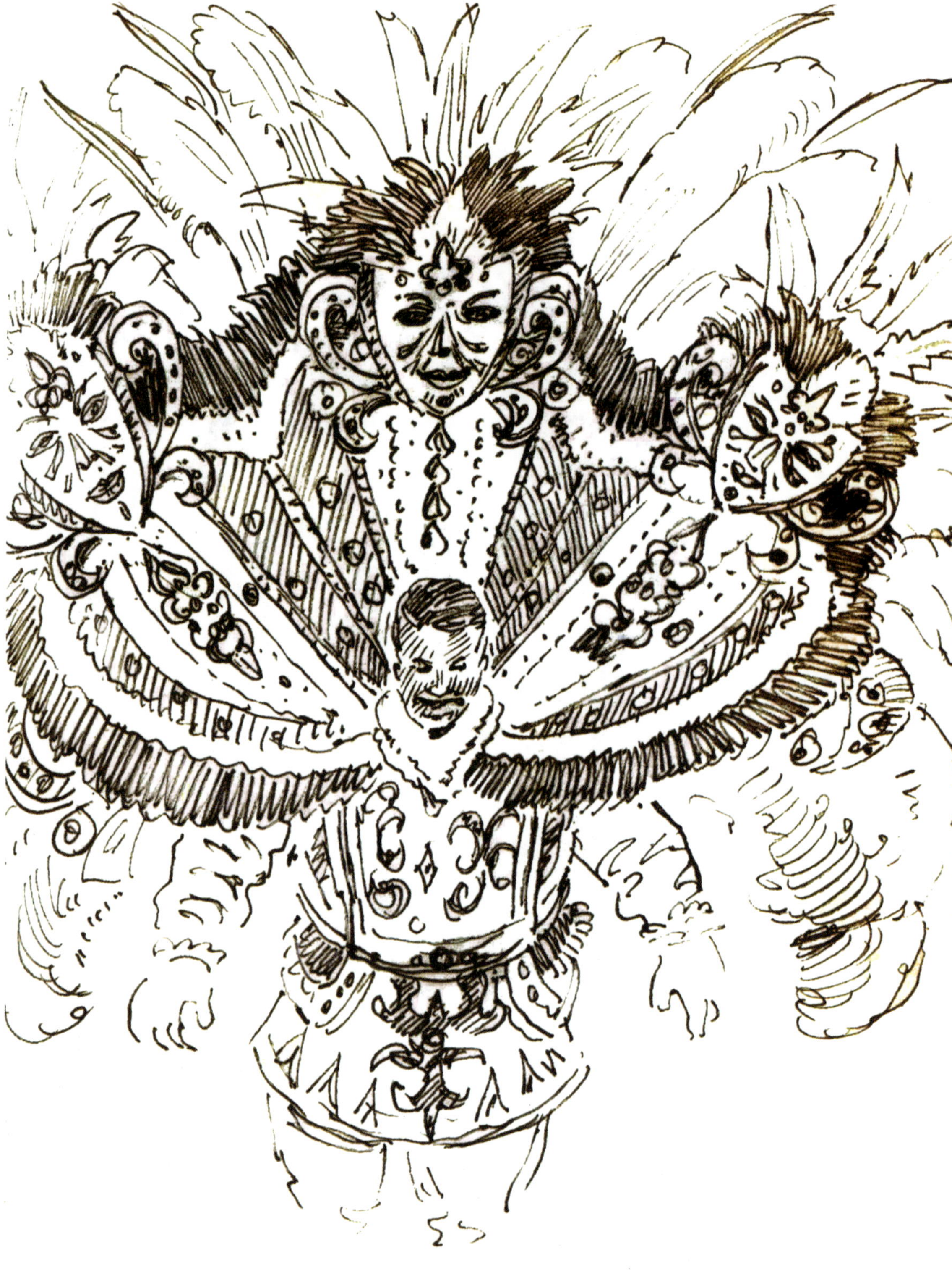

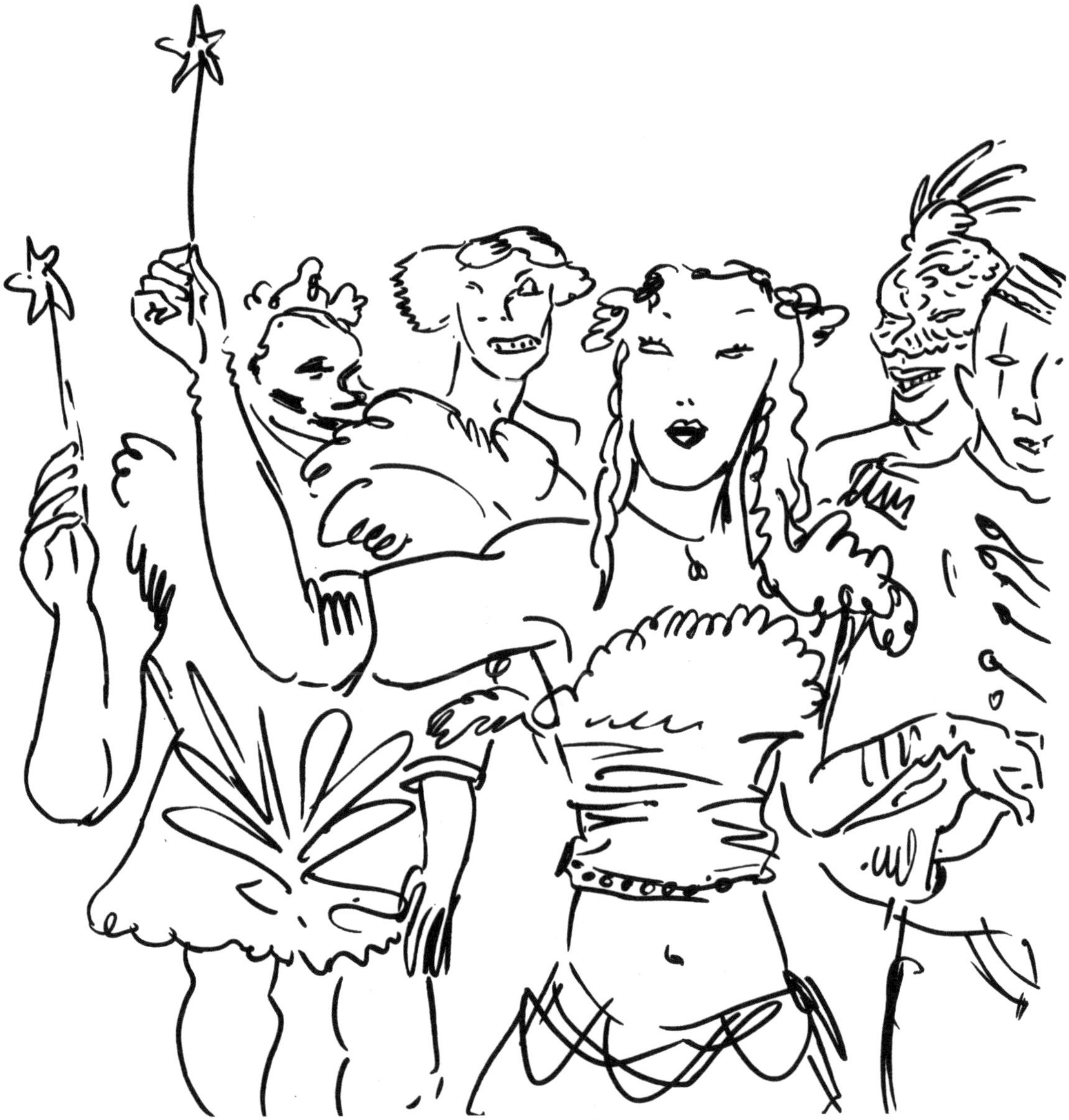

81

Fairies on Dauphine Street. The Zulu King (on left).

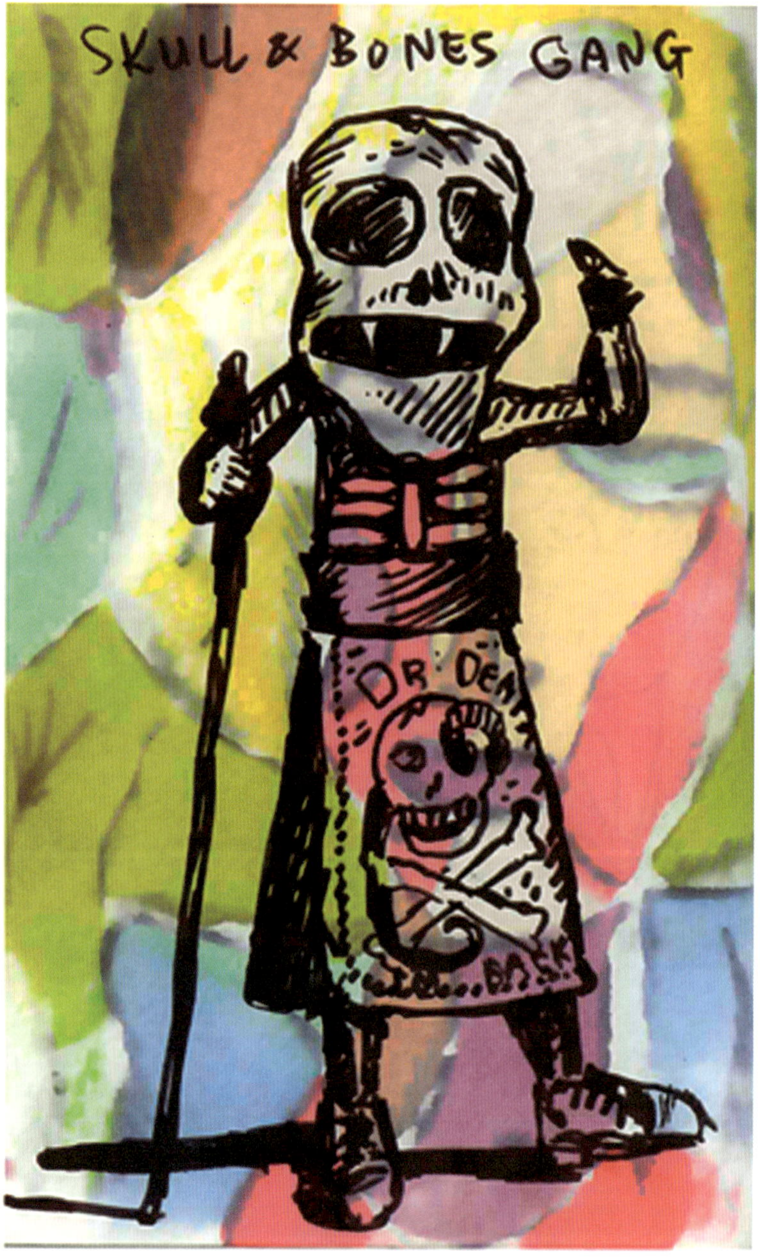
SKULL & BONES GANG

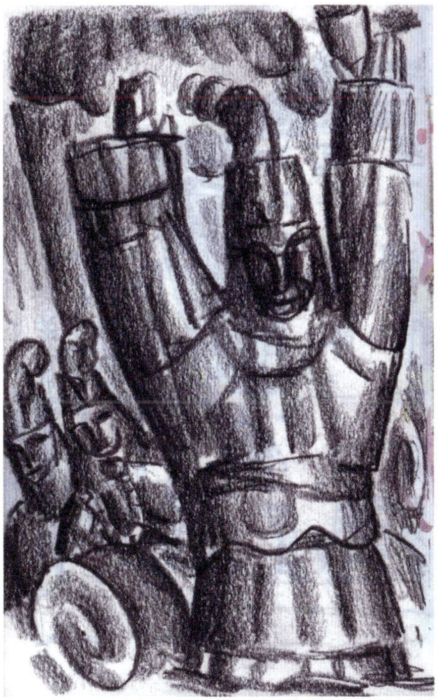

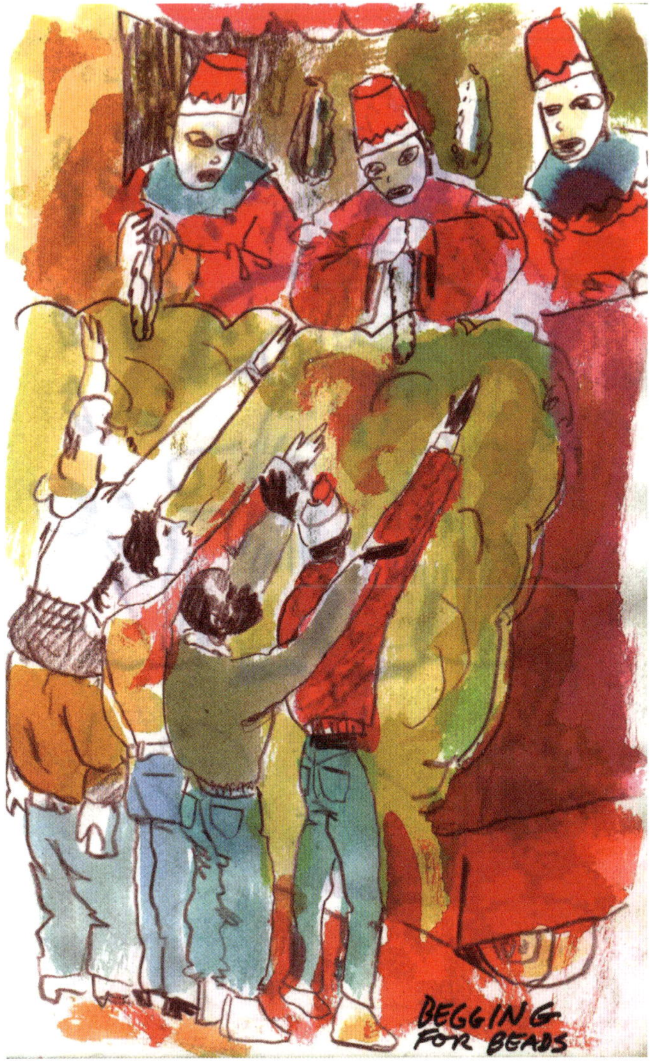





Catching plastic beads and doubloons as if they came from Tiffany's.

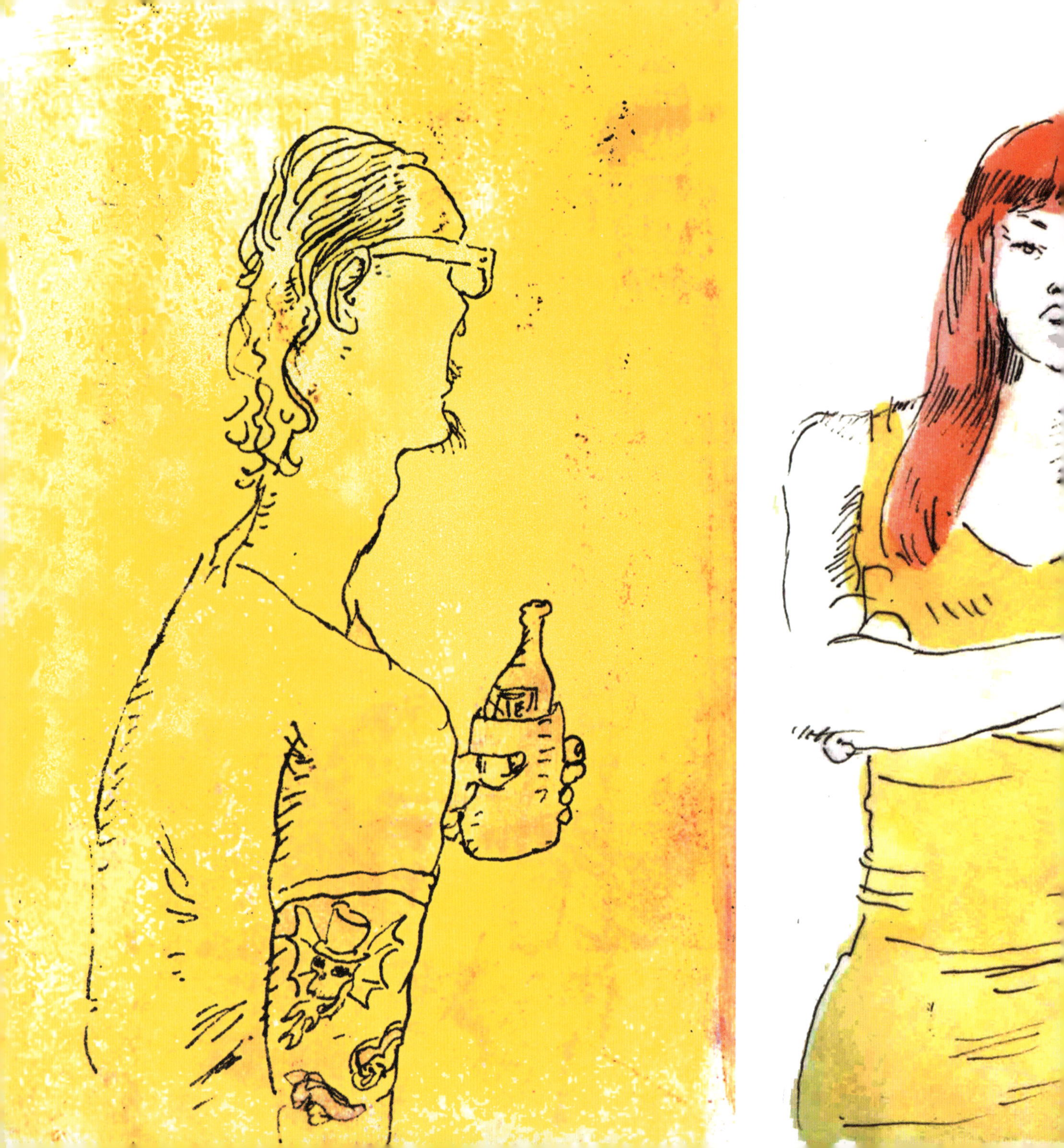

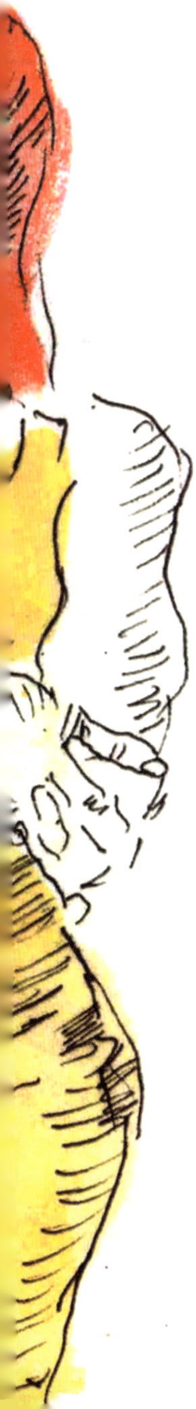

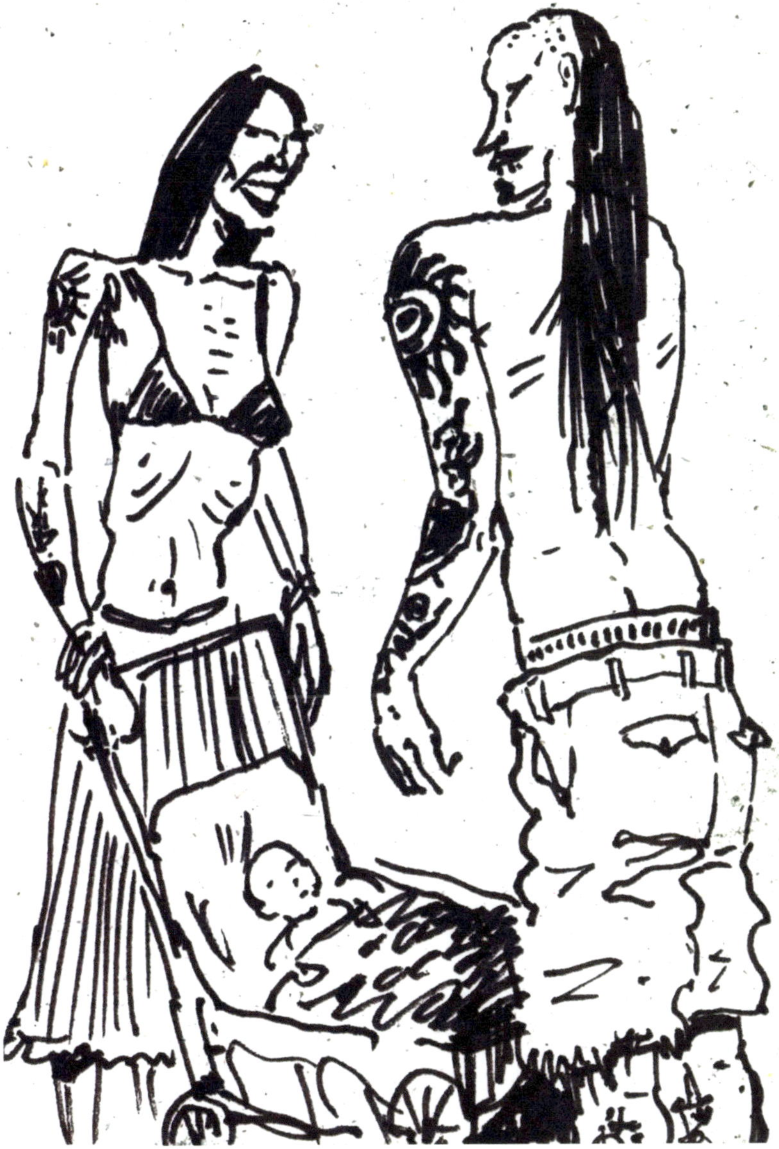

Goth family.

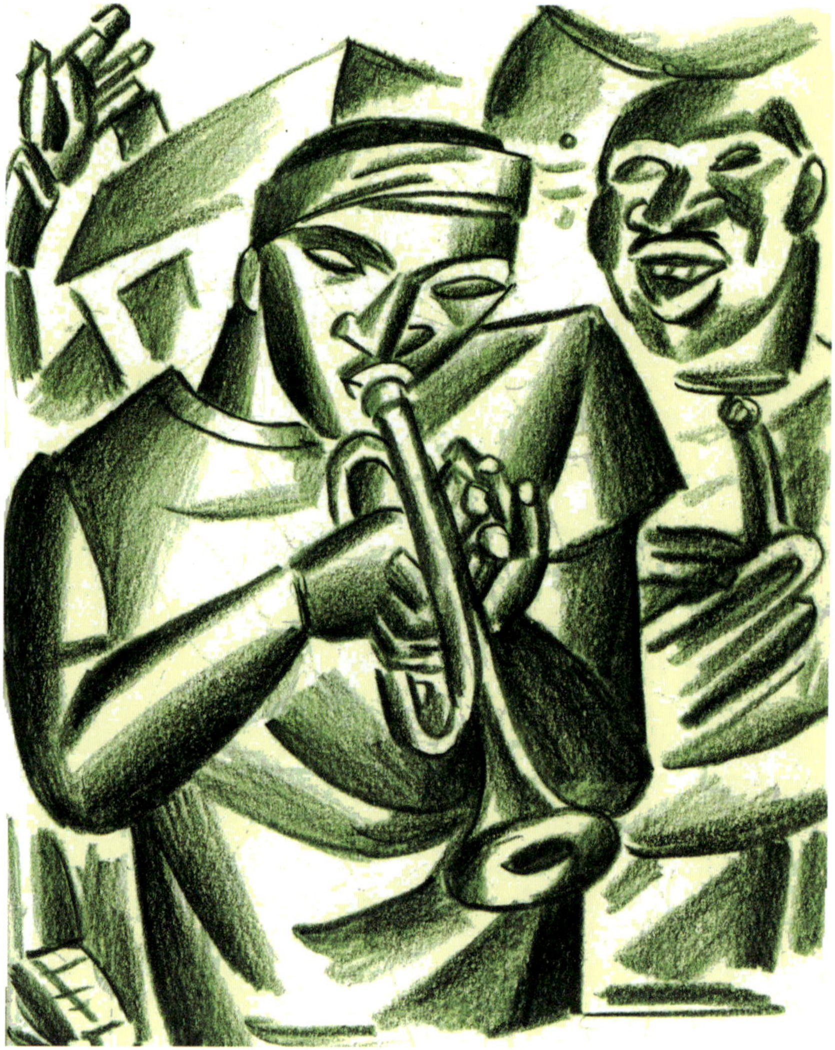

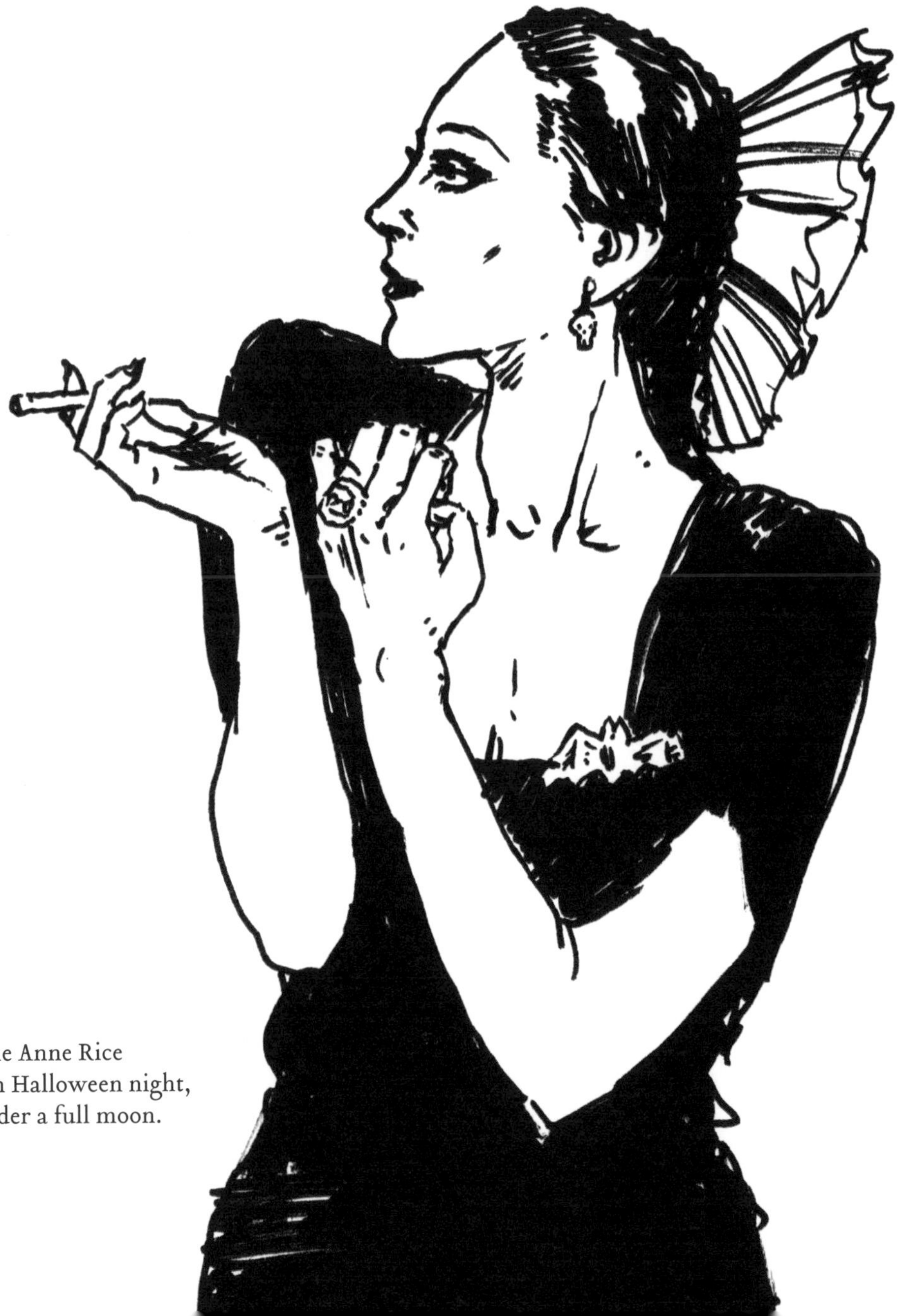

Vamp at the Anne Rice
Vampire Ball on Halloween night,
under a full moon.

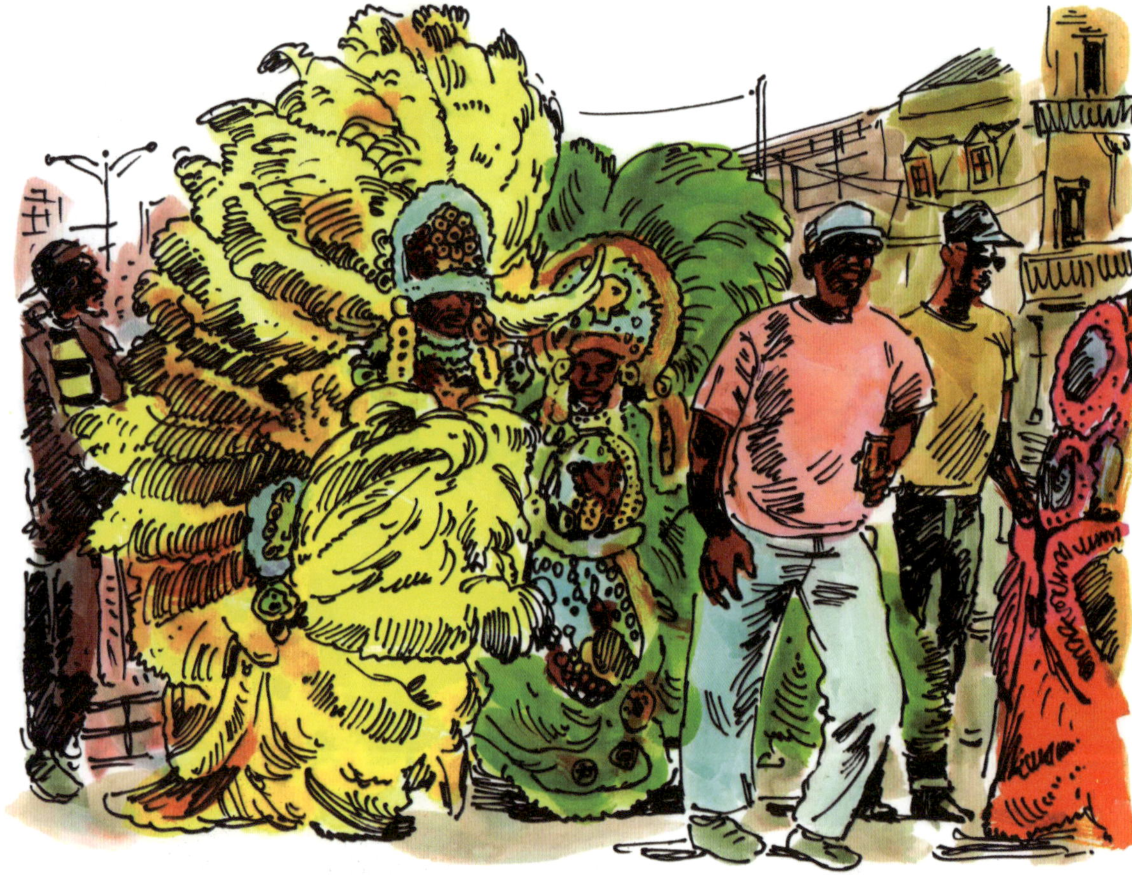



Technicolor magnificence of the Mardi Gras Indians on Carnival Day.
I can't find colors bright enough to describe the effect of sunlight on the fluttering feathered headdresses.
Montezuma would be proud.

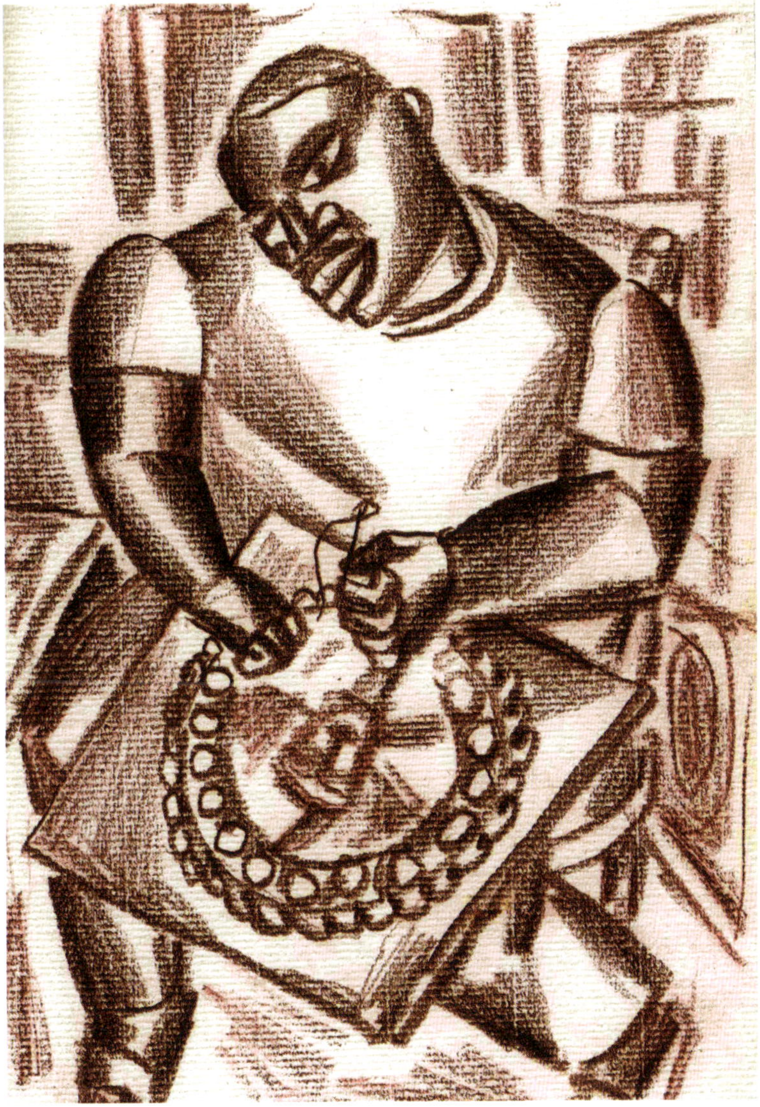



Larry Bannock, Chief of the Golden Star Hunters Mardi Gras Indians, and one of my best friends in New Orleans. He went missing right after Hurricane Katrina hit. He rode out the storm, until the levee broke. I located him a month later through contacts of contacts as I was making this book. I'm so glad he made it.

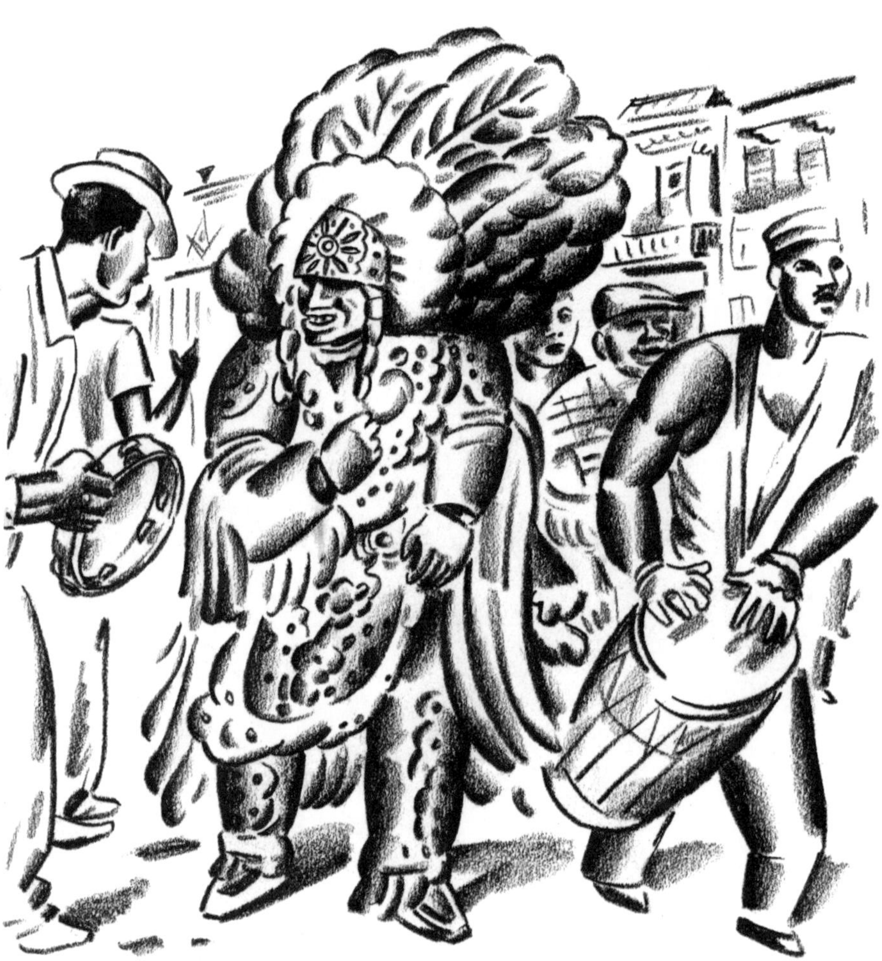



When he sings "Jack-A-Mo" the chief is the ruler of the holiday.

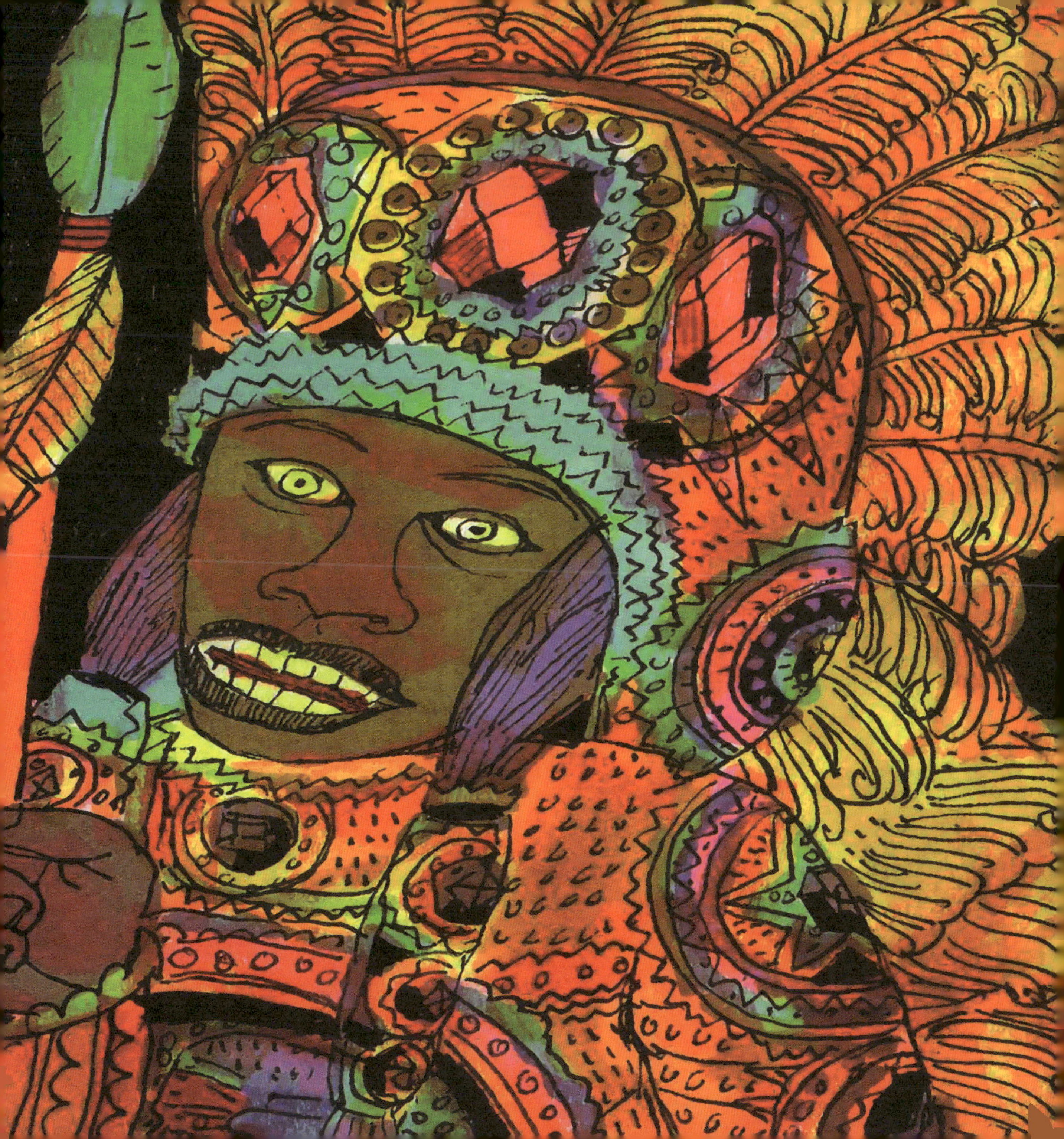

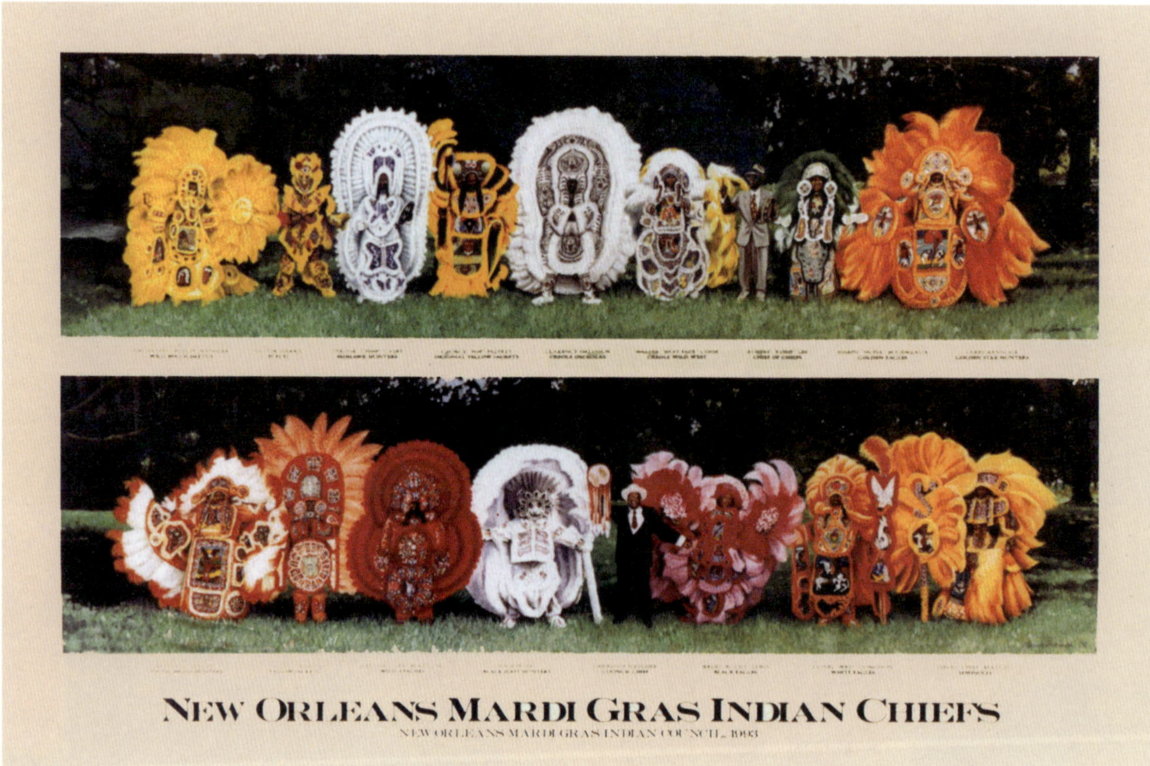




Portrait of seventeen of the Mardi Gras Big Chiefs (detail on right).

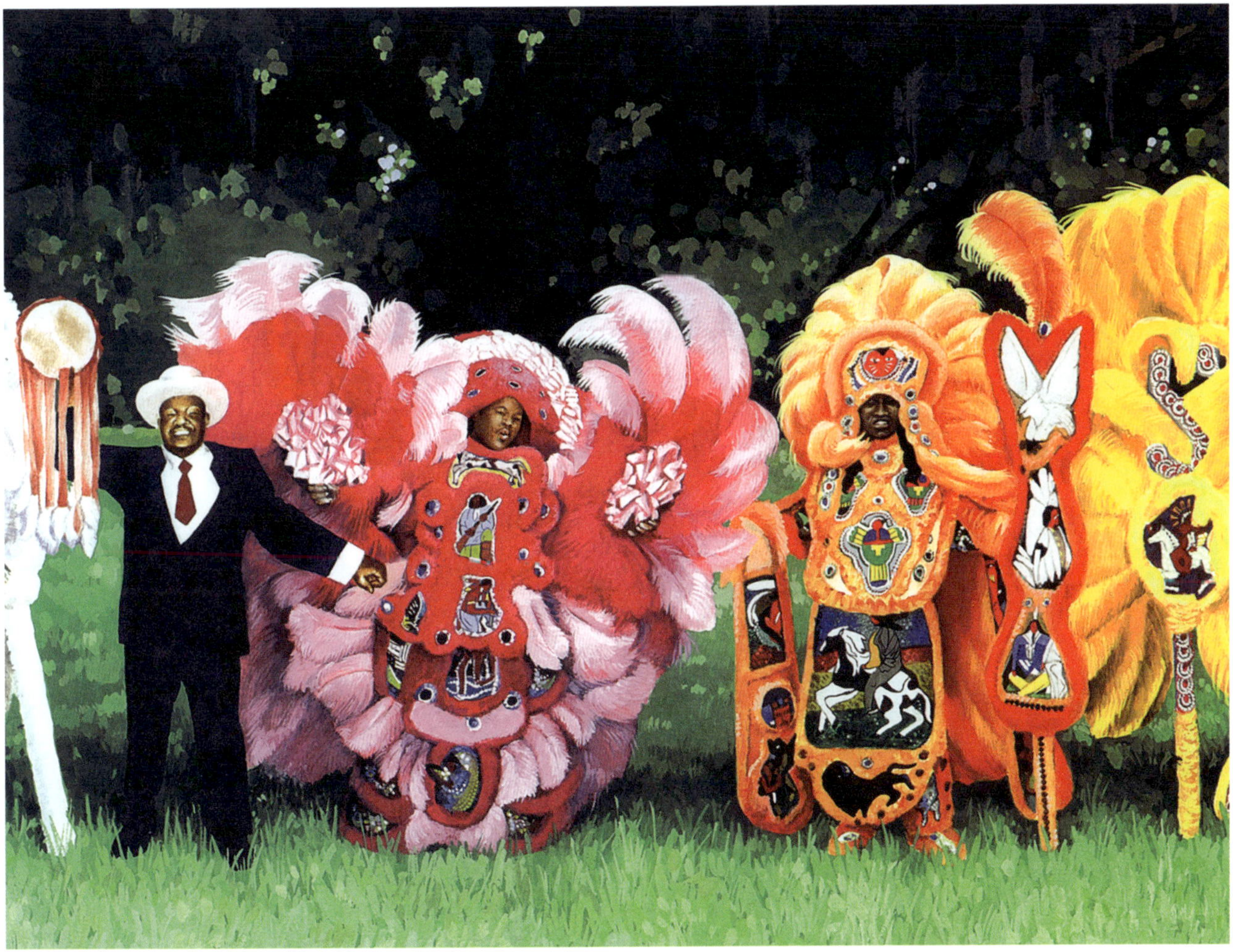

ETCHED IN MY MEMORY are the faces of the people of New Orleans. They are faces that are strong, vulnerable, warm, and friendly.

I've always enjoyed sketching these faces in the street while "on the run" so to speak. This requires a kind of visual shorthand with an emphasis on fluidity of line. I only get a quick glance before they're gone. The result is usually unfinished, and some portraits are idealized as I complete them from memory.

Every once in a while I'd give some homeless guy or a lovely girl a portrait—a symbol of the unspoken happiness we shared.

On the following pages are portraits of the people of New Orleans surrounding me in the days before Hurricane Katrina wiped the smiles off their faces.

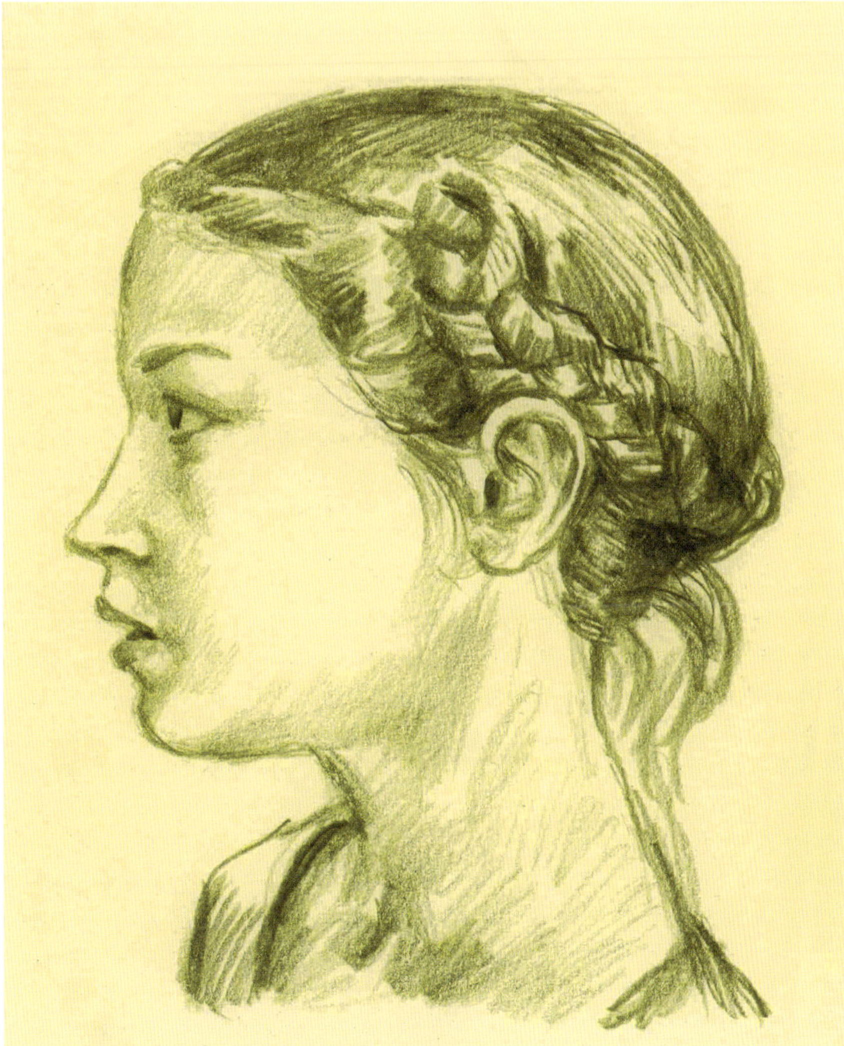

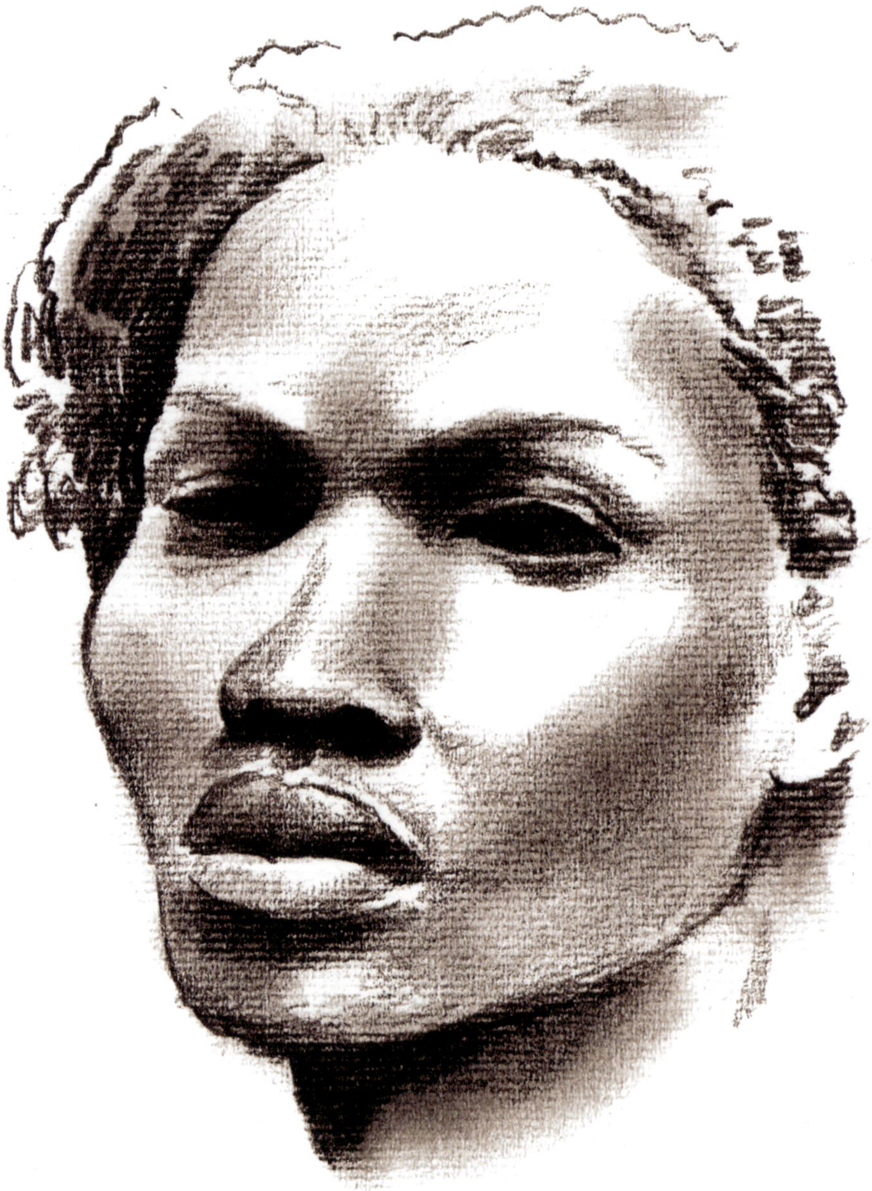

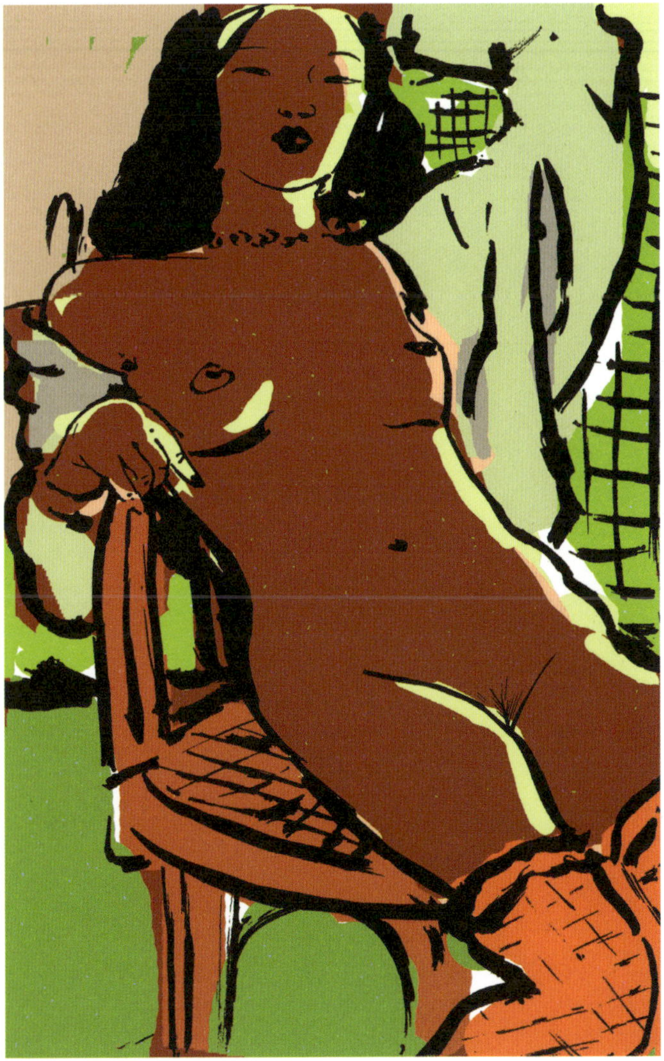

Creole girls.

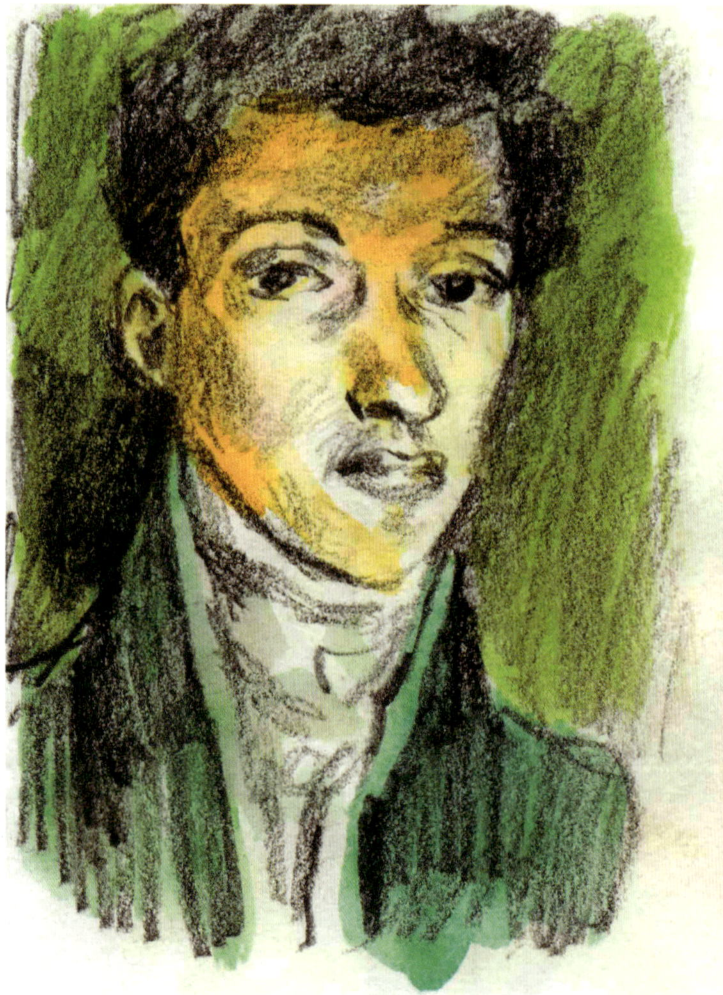

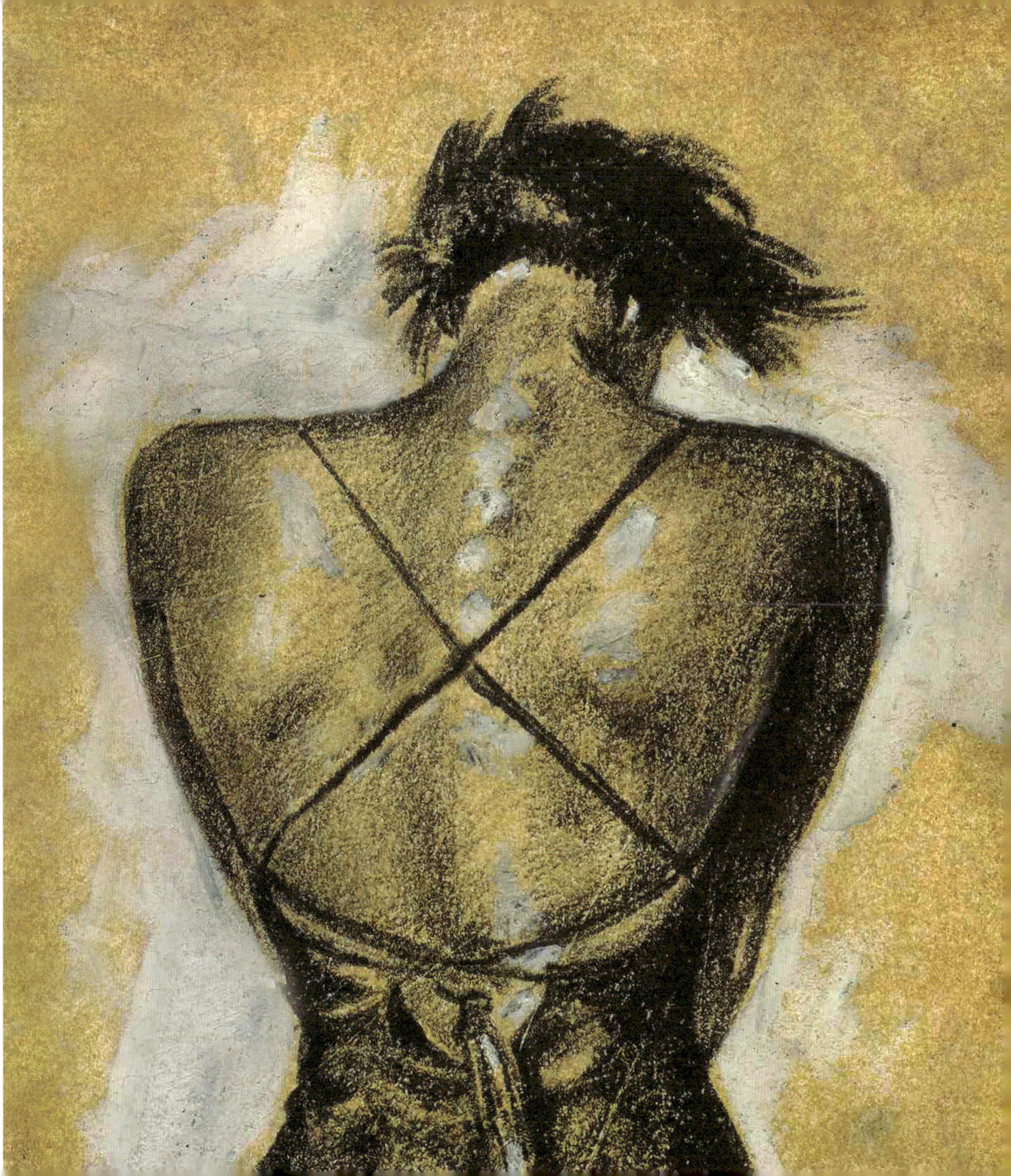

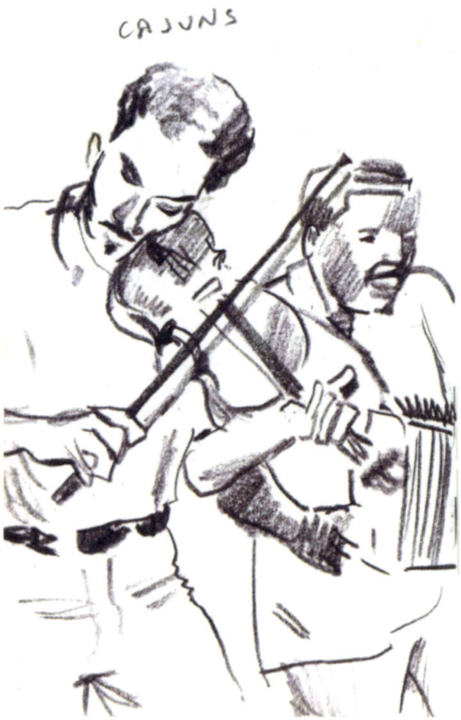
CAJUNS

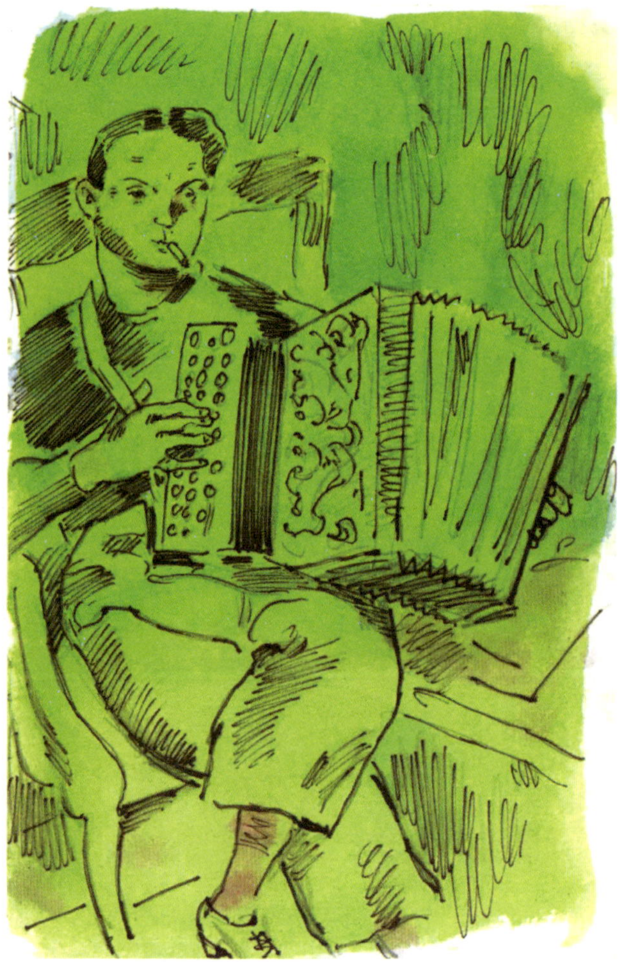

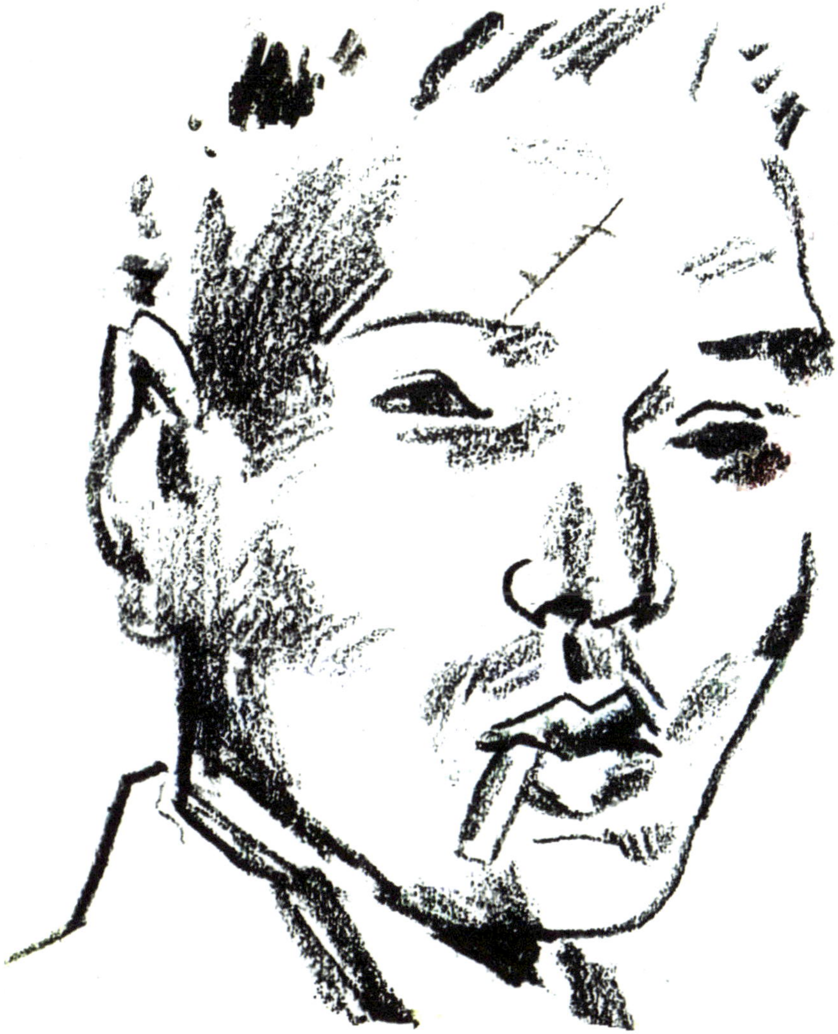

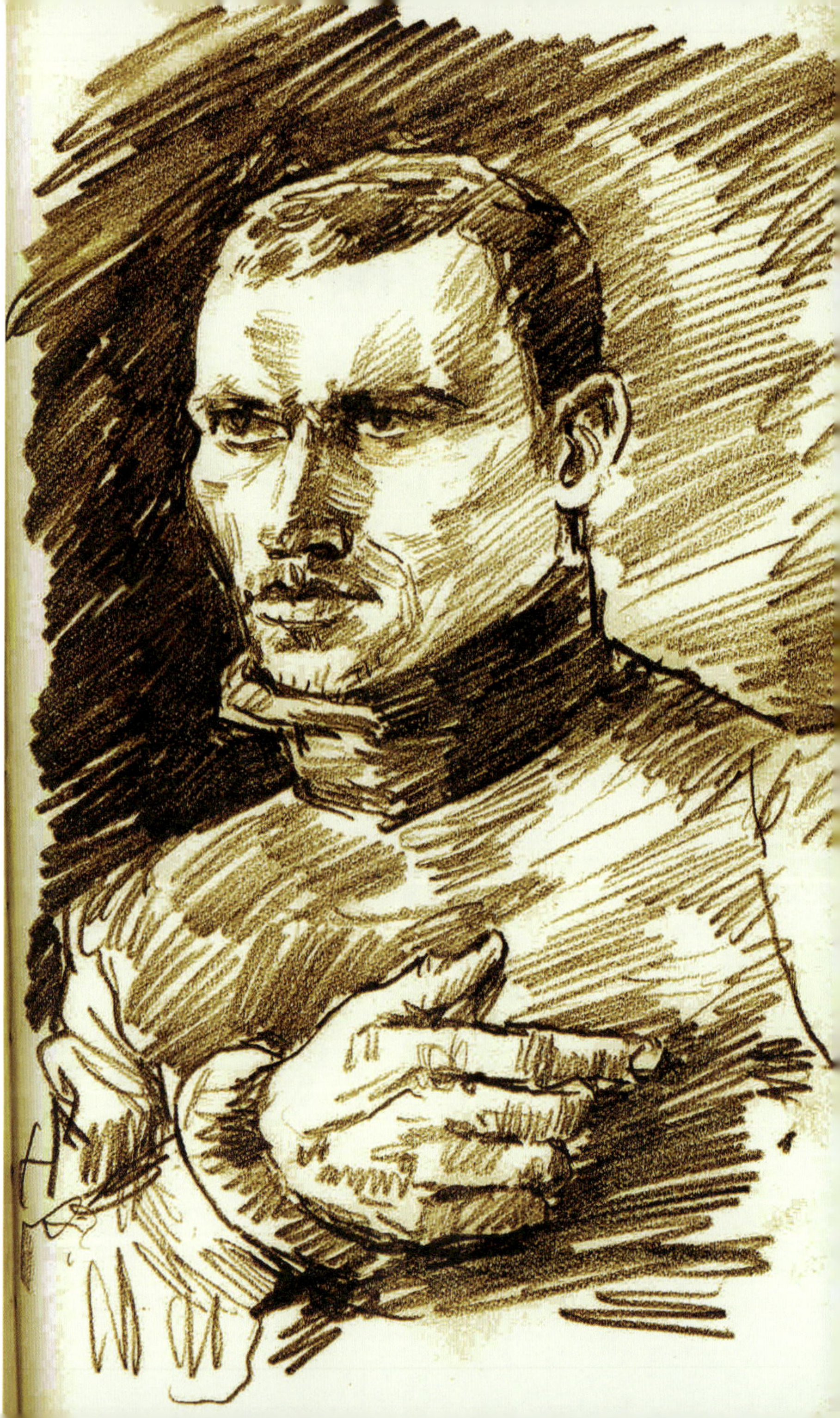

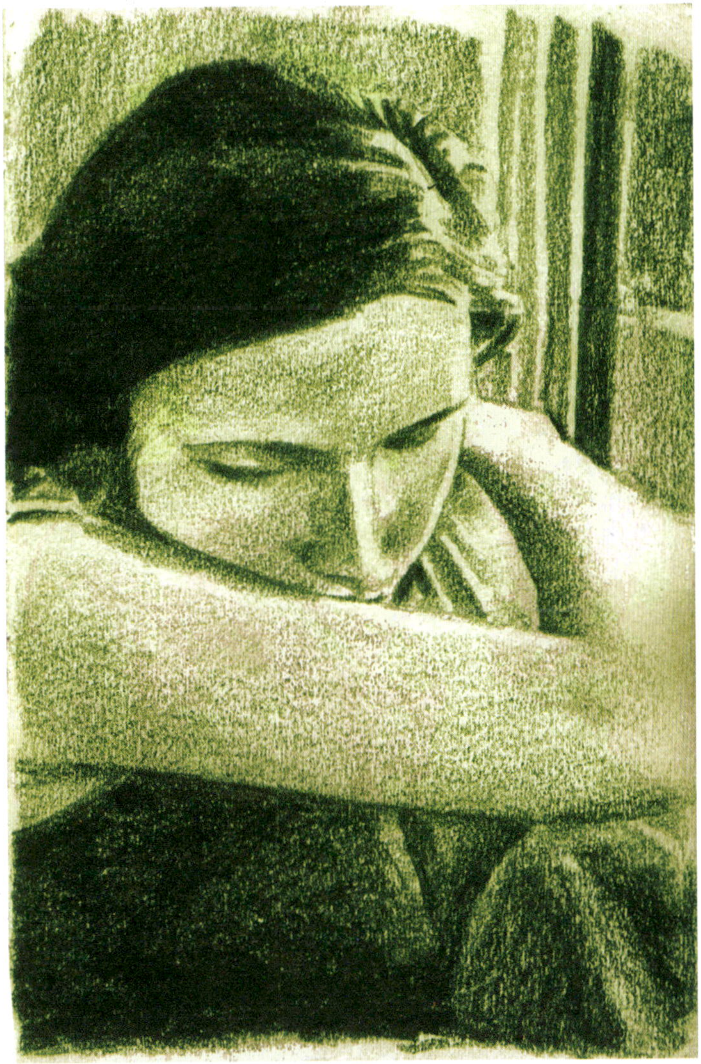

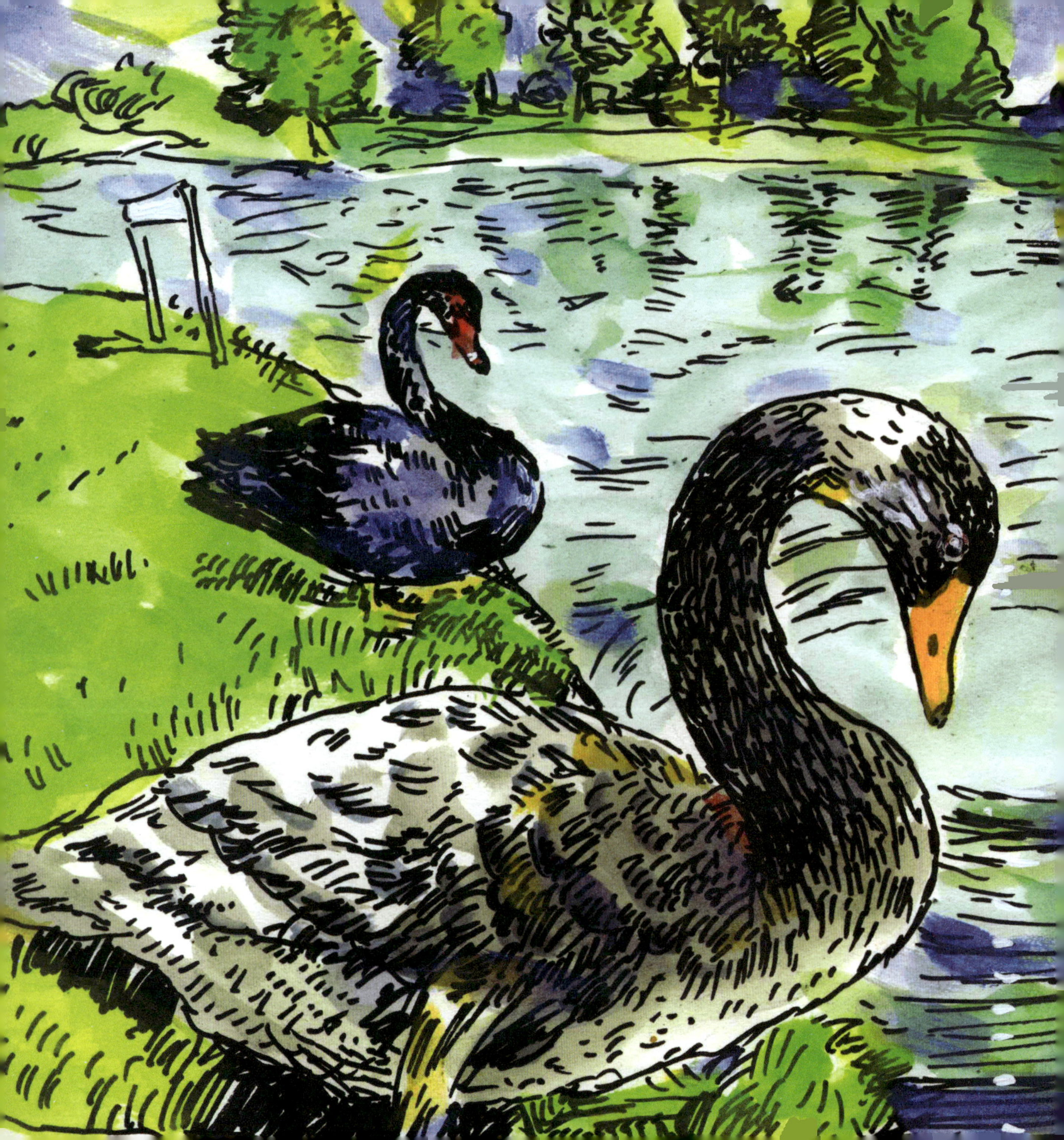

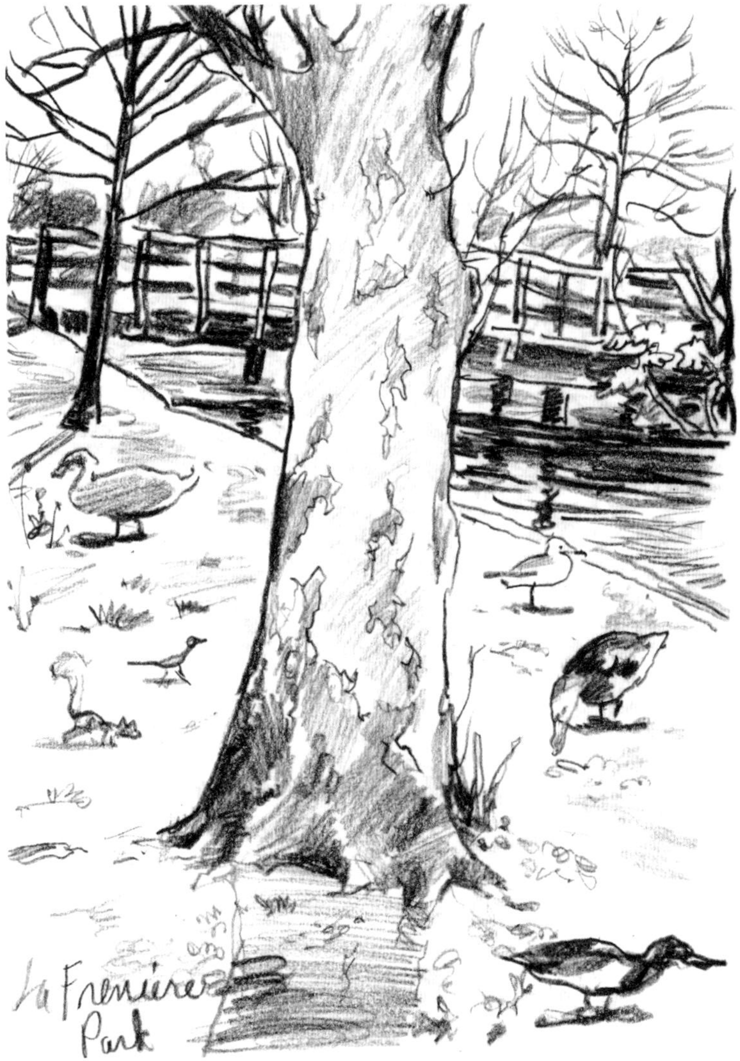
Park

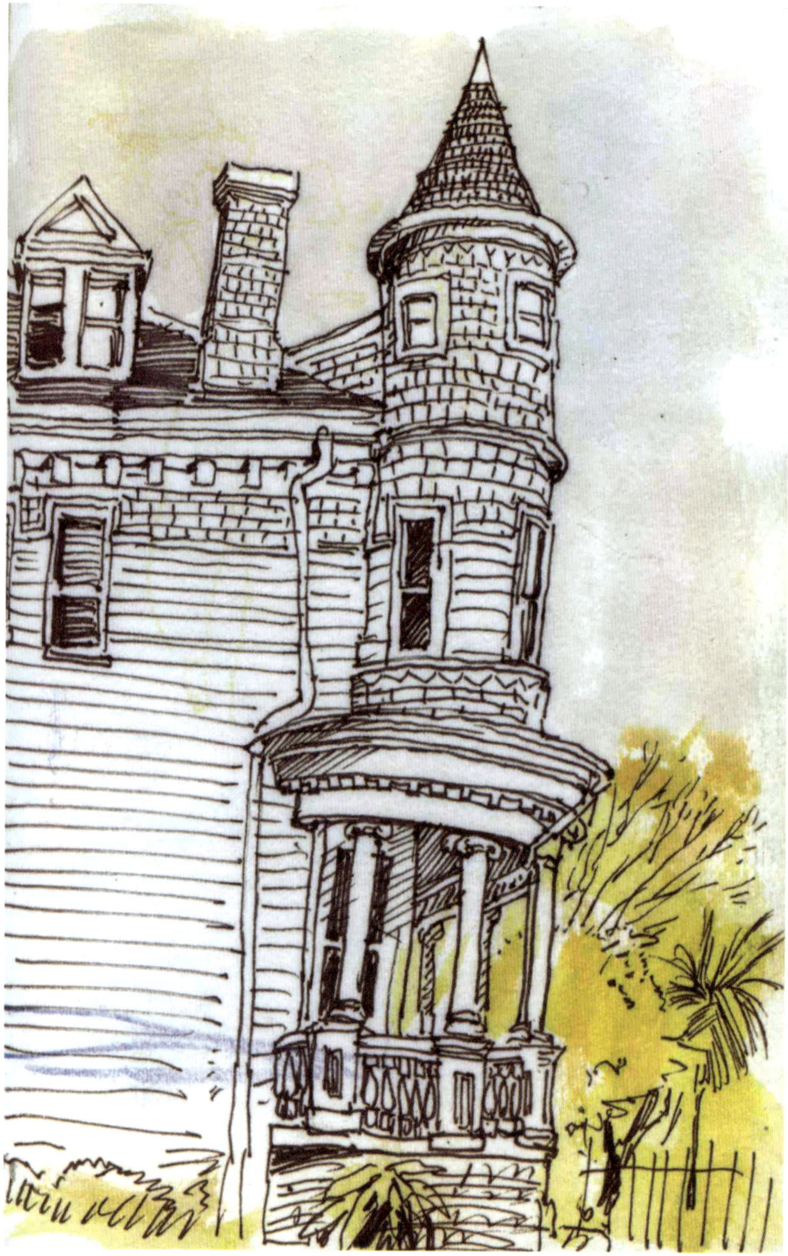

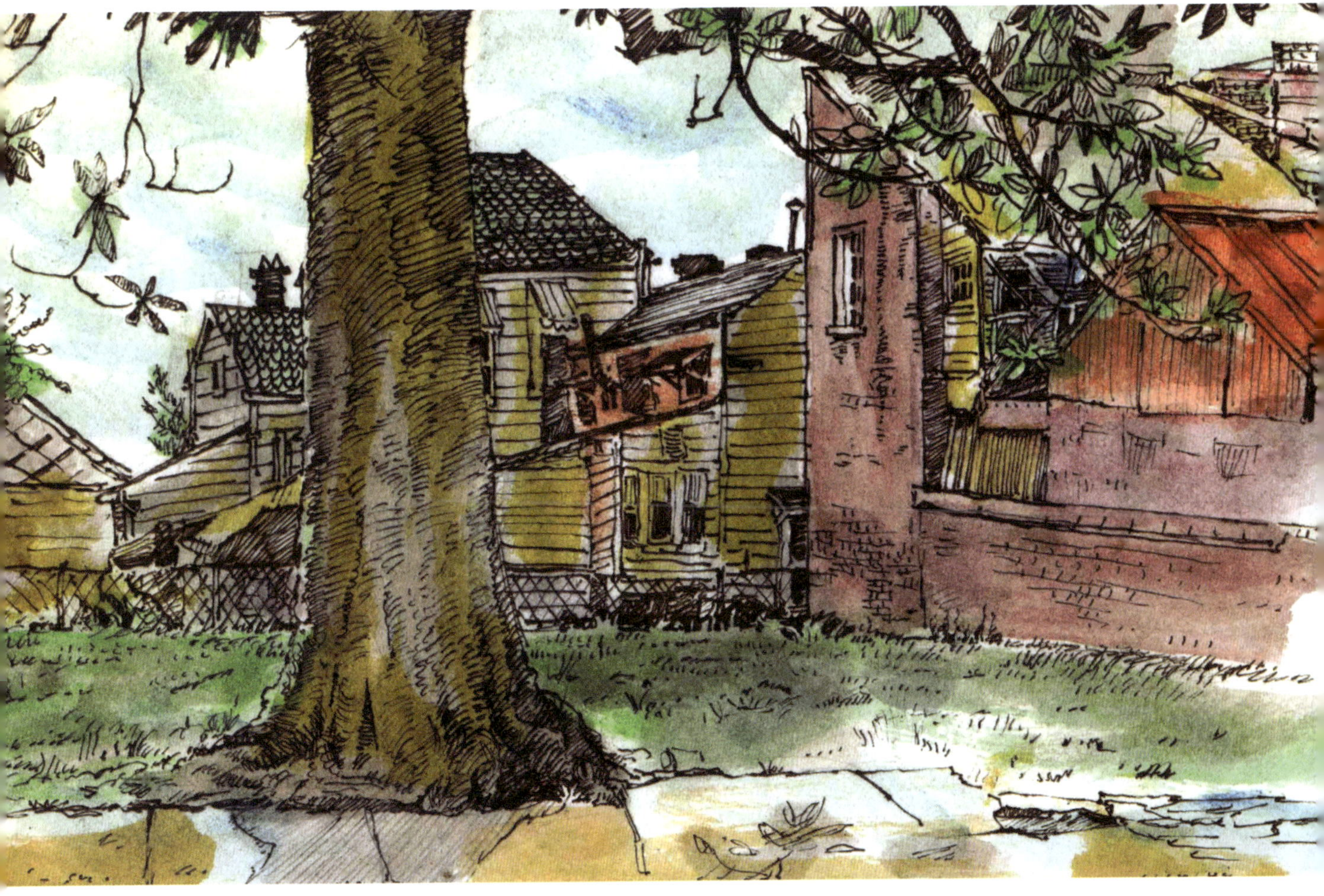

Uptown on Magazine Street.

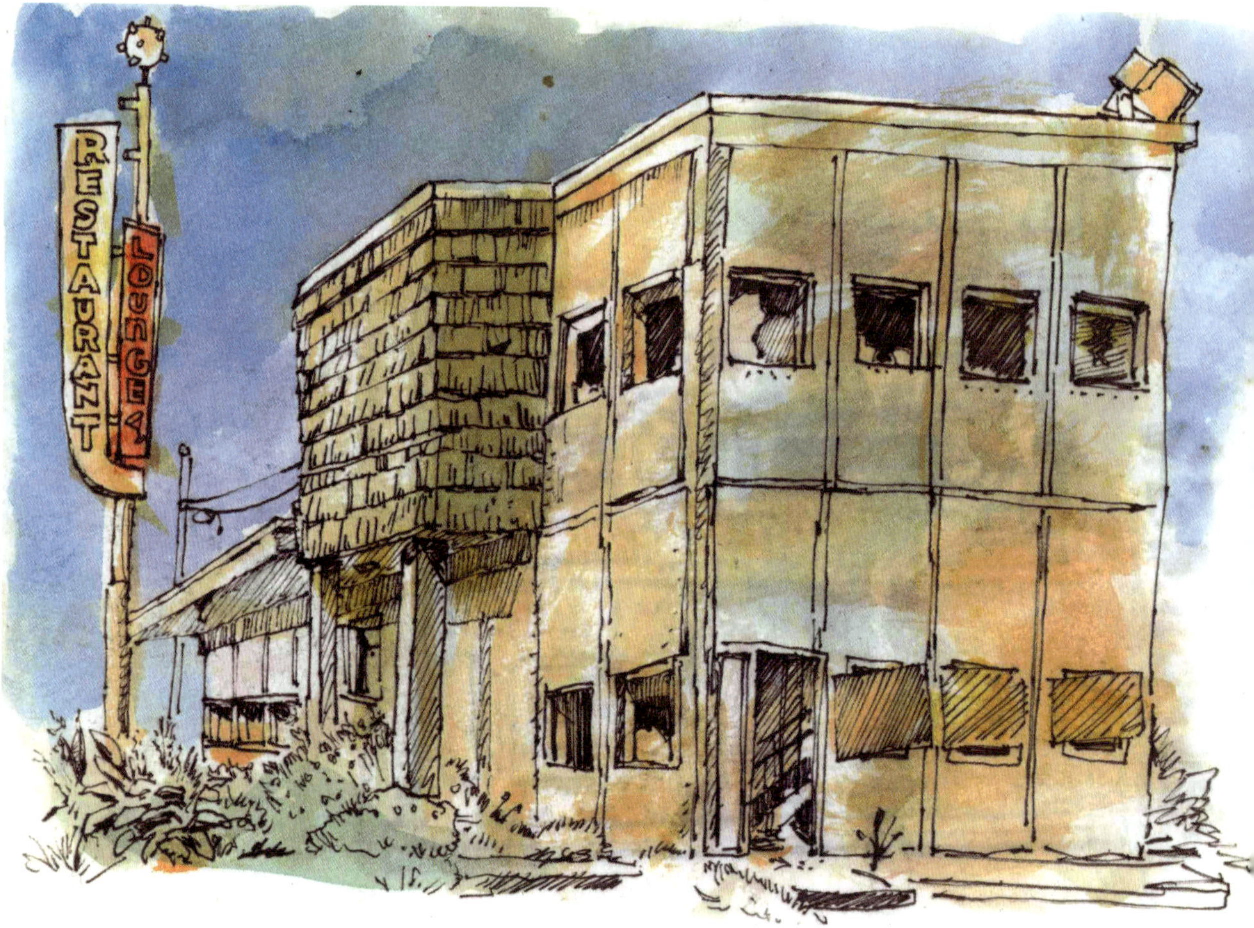




Abandoned motel on Highway 61.

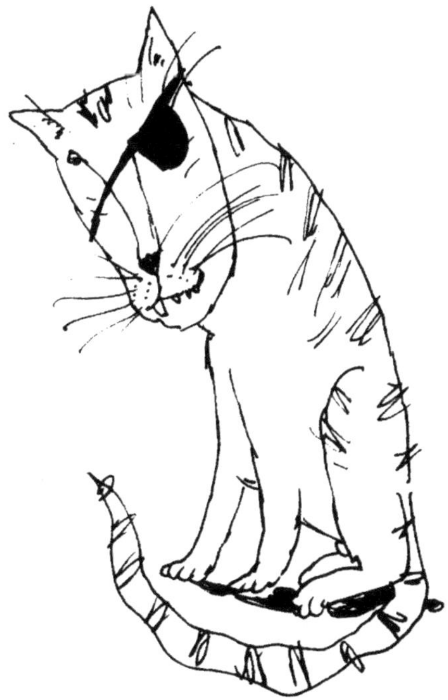

*I* DREW FEW PICTURES after Hurricane Katrina.

This one was drawn from memory—of the news images, not the flood itself. It was drawn on government handout papers while I was at a Red Cross facility sitting in one of many long lines of refugees—African-Americans, Cajuns, suburban people, and a few Vietnamese. All with stunned expressions.

I drew because I was exhausted, wanting to make sense of this loss, this sheer human tragedy.

We evacuated.

You can lose your house, your livelihood, and still be lucky compared to many. Especially those on the coast of Mississippi and the lower parishes.

To those who want to rebuild, I say "Good luck."

I was flung to an even stranger city—ultra modern Atlanta. It feels like fast forwarding a hundred years.

I wonder if I can ever go back.

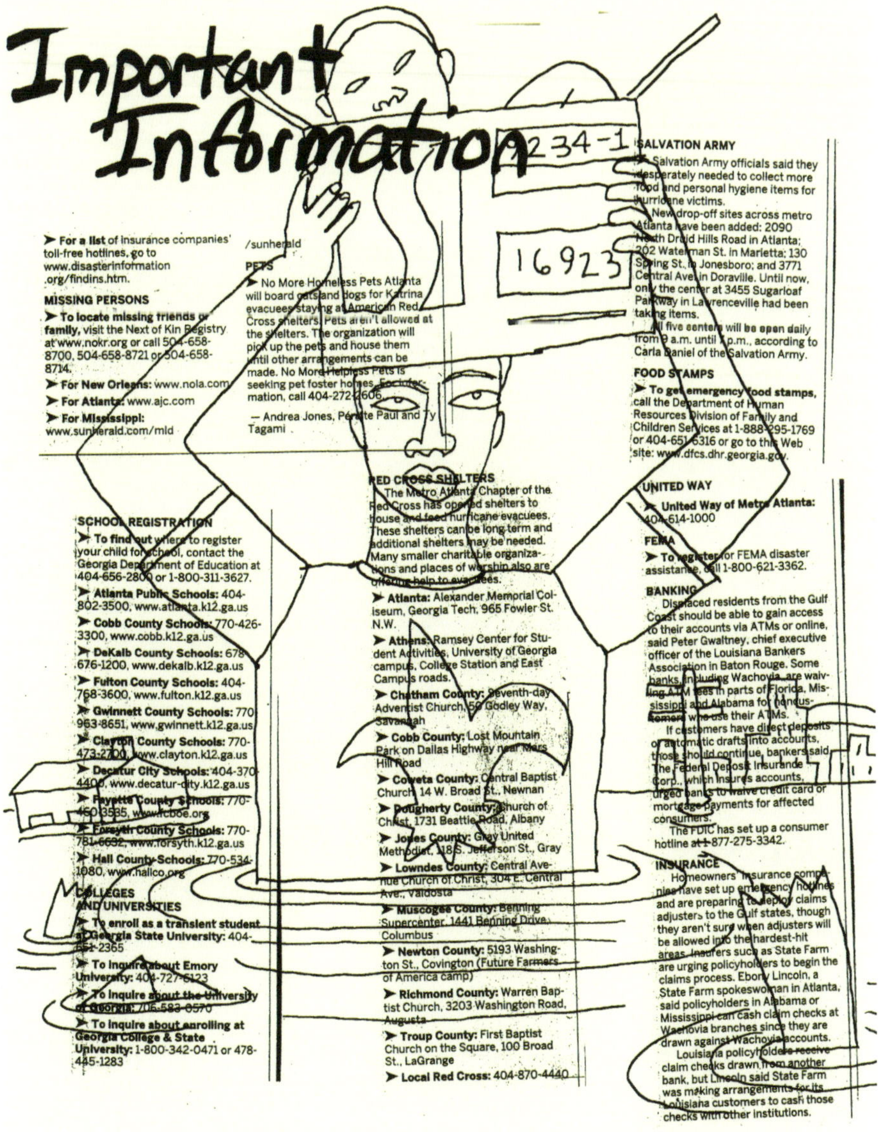
Important Information
234-1
16923
➤ For a list of insurance companies' toll-free hotlines, go to www.disasterinformation.org/findins.htm.
MISSING PERSONS
➤ To locate missing friends or family, visit the Next of Kin Registry at www.nokr.org or call 504-658-8700, 504-658-8721 or 504-658-8714.
➤ For New Orleans: www.nola.com
➤ For Atlanta: www.ajc.com
➤ For Mississippi: www.sunherald.com/mld/sunherald
PETS
➤ No More Homeless Pets Atlanta will board cats and dogs for Katrina evacuees staying at American Red Cross shelters. Pets aren't allowed at the shelters. The organization will pick up the pets and house them until other arrangements can be made. No More Helpless Pets is seeking pet foster homes. For information, call 404-272-2606.
— Andrea Jones, Pérette Paul and Ty Tagami
SALVATION ARMY
➤ Salvation Army officials said they desperately needed to collect more food and personal hygiene items for hurricane victims.
New drop-off sites across metro Atlanta have been added: 2090 North Druid Hills Road in Atlanta; 202 Waterman St. in Marietta; 130 Spring St. in Jonesboro; and 3771 Central Ave. in Doraville. Until now, only the center at 3455 Sugarloaf Parkway in Lawrenceville had been taking items.
All five centers will be open daily from 9 a.m. until 7 p.m., according to Carla Daniel of the Salvation Army.
FOOD STAMPS
➤ To get emergency food stamps, call the Department of Human Resources Division of Family and Children Services at 1-888-295-1769 or 404-651-6316 or go to this Web site: www.dfcs.dhr.georgia.gov.
SCHOOL REGISTRATION
➤ To find out where to register your child for school, contact the Georgia Department of Education at 404-656-2800 or 1-800-311-3627.
➤ Atlanta Public Schools: 404-802-3500, www.atlanta.k12.ga.us
➤ Cobb County Schools: 770-426-3300, www.cobb.k12.ga.us
➤ DeKalb County Schools: 678-676-1200, www.dekalb.k12.ga.us
➤ Fulton County Schools: 404-768-3600, www.fulton.k12.ga.us
➤ Gwinnett County Schools: 770-963-8651, www.gwinnett.k12.ga.us
➤ Clayton County Schools: 770-473-2700, www.clayton.k12.ga.us
➤ Decatur City Schools: 404-370-4400, www.decatur-city.k12.ga.us
➤ Fayette County Schools: 770-460-3535, www.fcboe.org
➤ Forsyth County Schools: 770-781-6632, www.forsyth.k12.ga.us
➤ Hall County Schools: 770-534-1080, www.hallco.org
COLLEGES AND UNIVERSITIES
➤ To enroll as a transient student at Georgia State University: 404-651-2365
➤ To inquire about Emory University: 404-727-6123
➤ To inquire about the University of Georgia: 706-583-0570
➤ To inquire about enrolling at Georgia College & State University: 1-800-342-0471 or 478-445-1283
RED CROSS SHELTERS
The Metro Atlanta Chapter of the Red Cross has opened shelters to house and feed hurricane evacuees. These shelters can be long-term and additional shelters may be needed. Many smaller charitable organizations and places of worship also are offering help to evacuees.
➤ Atlanta: Alexander Memorial Coliseum, Georgia Tech, 965 Fowler St. N.W.
➤ Athens: Ramsey Center for Student Activities, University of Georgia campus, College Station and East Campus roads.
➤ Chatham County: Seventh-day Adventist Church, 50 Godley Way, Savannah
➤ Cobb County: Lost Mountain Park on Dallas Highway near Mars Hill Road
➤ Coweta County: Central Baptist Church, 14 W. Broad St., Newnan
➤ Dougherty County: Church of Christ, 1731 Beattie Road, Albany
➤ Jones County: Gray United Methodist, 118 S. Jefferson St., Gray
➤ Lowndes County: Central Avenue Church of Christ, 304 E. Central Ave., Valdosta
➤ Muscogee County: Benning Supercenter, 1441 Benning Drive, Columbus
➤ Newton County: 5193 Washington St., Covington (Future Farmers of America camp)
➤ Richmond County: Warren Baptist Church, 3203 Washington Road, Augusta
➤ Troup County: First Baptist Church on the Square, 100 Broad St., LaGrange
➤ Local Red Cross: 404-870-4440
UNITED WAY
➤ United Way of Metro Atlanta: 404-614-1000
FEMA
➤ To register for FEMA disaster assistance, call 1-800-621-3362.
BANKING
Displaced residents from the Gulf Coast should be able to gain access to their accounts via ATMs or online, said Peter Gwaltney, chief executive officer of the Louisiana Bankers Association in Baton Rouge. Some banks, including Wachovia, are waiving ATM fees in parts of Florida, Mississippi and Alabama for noncustomers who use their ATMs.
If customers have direct deposits or automatic drafts into accounts, those should continue, bankers said. The Federal Deposit Insurance Corp., which insures accounts, urged banks to waive credit card or mortgage payments for affected consumers.
The FDIC has set up a consumer hotline at 1-877-275-3342.
INSURANCE
Homeowners' insurance companies have set up emergency hotlines and are preparing to deploy claims adjusters to the Gulf states, though they aren't sure when adjusters will be allowed into the hardest-hit areas. Insurers such as State Farm are urging policyholders to begin the claims process. Ebony Lincoln, a State Farm spokeswoman in Atlanta, said policyholders in Alabama or Mississippi can cash claim checks at Wachovia branches since they are drawn against Wachovia accounts.
Louisiana policyholders receive claim checks drawn from another bank, but Lincoln said State Farm was making arrangements for its Louisiana customers to cash those checks with other institutions.

Sweet Home New Orleans.